50 wonderful ways to be a SINGLE-PARENT FAMILY

BARRY G. GINSBERG, PH.D.

Foreword by Roberta Israeloff

New Harbinger Publications, Inc.

Publisher's Note

This publication is designed to provide accurate and authoritative information in regard to the subject matter covered. It is sold with the understanding that the publisher is not engaged in rendering psychological, financial, legal, or other professional services. If expert assistance or counseling is needed, the services of a competent professional should be sought.

Distributed in the U.S.A. by Publishers Group West; in Canada by Raincoast Books; in Great Britain by Hi Marketing, Ltd.; in South Africa by Real Books, Ltd.; in Australia by Boobook; and in New Zealand by Tandem Press.

Copyright © 2002 by Barry G. Ginsberg
New Harbinger Publications, Inc.
5674 Shattuck Avenue
Oakland, CA 94609

Cover design by Amy Shoup
Cover image by Buzz Bailey/The Image Bank
Edited by Carole Honeychurch
Text design by Michele Waters

ISBN 1-57224-308-2 Paperback

All Rights Reserved

Printed in the United States of America

New Harbinger Publications' Web site address: www.newharbinger.com

04   03   02

10   9   8   7   6   5   4   3   2   1

First printing

This book is dedicated to my mother, Leah Schwartz Ginsberg Epstein, a remarkable woman and single parent.

Contents

	Preface	ix
	Introduction	1
Part I	*Coping with Transition and Change*	5
	1. Look for Positives	6
	2. Develop a "Can-Do" Attitude	8
	3 Keep Your Strengths in Mind	10
	4. Meet Your Children's Needs	12
	5. Take Good Care of Yourself	14
	6. Learn to Juggle	16
	7. Share the Load: You Can't Do Everything	18
	8. Decisions: A Family Affair	20
	9. Build a Support Network	22

	10. Involve the Other Parent	24
	11. Develop Rituals and Traditions	26
	12. Learn to Manage Your Stress	28
Part II	*Talking and Listening*	**31**
	13. Show Respect	32
	14. Make Time to Talk	34
	15. Pay Attention to Feelings	36
	16. Know Yourself	38
	17. Say What You Mean	42
	18. Show Understanding	44
	19. Learn to Actively Listen	46
	20. Talking with Young Chidren	48
	21. Talking with Adolescents	50
	22. Talking with Those Close to You	52
	23. Talking to the Other Parent	54
	24. Talking Creates Change	56
Part III	*Working and Playing*	**59**
	25. Juggle Work and Home	60
	26. Handle Work Pressures at Home	62
	27. We Are a Team	66
	28. Have Regular Family Meetings	68
	29. Be Realistic about Household Chores	70
	30. Manage Schoolwork and Homework	72
	31. Balance Work and Play	74
	32. Importance of Play	76

33.	Play Together	78
34.	Take Time for Play	80
35.	Create a Special Playtime with Each Child	82
36.	Celebrate Holidays and Other Occasions	86
37.	Get Ready to Date	88
38.	Share Your Playtime with Others	90

Part IV *Getting Along* — 93

39.	Find Common Ground	94
40.	Learn to Accept Differences	96
41.	Be Flexible	98
42.	Negotiate Clear Boundaries	100
43.	Be Realistic about Rules	102
44.	Use Your Power Constructively	104
45.	Make Conflict Useful	108
46.	Getting Along as a Whole Family	110
47.	Getting Along with the Other Parent	112
48.	Getting Along with Young Children	114
49.	Getting Along with Adolescents	116
50.	Getting Along with Your Extended Family	118

Conclusion — 121

Preface

Nothing's harder than being a parent. The task at hand—the responsibility to raise good children—presents enormous challenges on its own. But add to it our anxiety—"Am I doing a good enough job? Can I do better? Did I handle that situation right?"—and the job becomes, at times, crushingly hard.

It's Dr. Barry Ginsberg's gift to ease our burden, and as a result, to make us believe that we can not only succeed as parents, but also thrive.

Dr. Ginsberg doesn't represent the role of parent as simpler than it is; rather, he is able to explain difficult concepts and interactions in basic terms without reducing their complexity. While Dr. Ginsberg's vision is realistic in terms of what parents can actually accomplish, it's also rooted in an optimistic view of human nature. He is convinced that with practice, patience, and good intentions, we can become the parents we want to be. Honest self-examination is at the root of this conviction. Yet his advice is eminently behavioral and sensible. He also proposes a set of values that are essential to having a good relationship with anyone: "Talk to each other. Respect each other. Listen to each other. Say what you mean and pay attention to how you feel. Take responsibility for yourself. Have family meetings. Set ground rules." These are principles we all know but sometimes forget or overlook. Remember them, Dr. Ginsberg urges us, for they themselves are our best resource. His confidence is contagious.

Every suggestion he offers stems from these values. To implement his advice isn't always easy. But like the best kind of coach, one who really has your welfare at heart, Dr. Ginsberg urges patience. "Take the time to read this book and digest its meaning, practice, and you'll get it," he tell us time and time again.

This book espouses a ground-up approach to parenting. As he explains, parents who know themselves have the assurance to know their children. He describes an emotional climate in which we all take responsibility for ourselves and then move forward to engage with others, whether it's our children, ex-spouses, friends, or members of our families of origin.

Dr. Ginsberg also suggests that we start with the basics and move on to complexity gradually. For instance, in order to know yourself more thoroughly, he encourages you to first decide if the feelings you have are good or bad. Only after that distinction has been made do you move on to elaborate. It's a plan so simple that you think it can't possible work, not with all the complexity with which you have to cope. But it does work.

Dr. Ginsberg is a parent as well as a psychologist. Throughout the book, you will hear both voices talking to you. Soon you'll hear yourselves talking and thinking differently than you ever did before. This book has helped me to be a better parent. Even my kids notice the difference. Yours will, too.

—Roberta Israeloff
past contributing editor of *Parenting* magazine

Most people would agree that family is what makes our lives meaningful, our most valuable resource. Family is multidimensional: it's what we're born into, develop out of, and continue to create throughout our lifetimes. Family carries on long after we are gone.

But our idea of family changes over time. In the sixty years since the end of World War II, the American family has undergone a huge transition. Think of what we expect of men and women. In the past, men worked outside the home and women worked within. Today, men and women are moving toward having more equivalent roles. As more women join the workforce, men have taken on more household and childcare responsibilities. Traditionally, women have been responsible for family cohesiveness and emotional expressiveness, but even this is changing. Though many men are embarrassed by expressing feelings and may withdraw into their "caves," many others are softening. They are feeling more comfortable talking about their emotions and seem less defensive about their masculinity.

But more than roles are changing. In recent years, the very definition of what constitutes a family has become broader and more diverse. Because of the increase in the rates of divorce and separation, today's family often includes children, stepchildren, and half-siblings; husbands, wives, ex-husbands and ex-wives; parents and stepparents; and a host of extended family members including grandparents, aunts, uncles, cousins and in-laws.

It's also true that the number of single-parent families is on the rise. According to 2000 Census figures, the number of families headed by single mothers has increased 25 percent since 1990, to more than 7.5 million households. The number of single fathers has also increased; single fathers now head more than two million families.

Whether the family is headed by a mother, father, or grandparent, single-parent families share many strengths and challenges. Among the important strengths derived from being part of a single-parent family is learning to work together. This fosters resilience, independence, and competence. One of the foremost challenges is learning to become more flexible in order to be able to confront new and changing circumstances while maintaining important values. Like all parents, single parents need to help their children be strong, optimistic, and enthusiastic about life, and to develop good self-concepts, good relationships, and good coping skills.

Single parents can achieve these goals by adhering to certain principles, attitudes, and methods that are important to all families and which can be adapted and modified to fit their circumstances. What's most important is to recognize that you can grow and develop strong, positive, constructive, and emotionally connected lives together, no matter what form your family might take. *50 Wonderful Ways to Be a Single Parent Family* is dedicated to this value.

Part I
Coping with Transition and Change

1. Look for Positives

No matter how bleak situations may appear, you can always find positives. When we look for positives, our spirits are lifted and we can cope better. After all, it's the positives that enrich our lives. The best positives are those feelings we have when we consider how much we love our kids and others close to us and how much they love us.

Think back, for example, to a time when parenting seemed like an overwhelming task. Perhaps this happened when you first became a single-parent. Obviously, it took some time to recover your equilibrium. But by now, if things have stabilized, your family has been transformed into a working single-parent family. With some time and consistent work on your part, the underlying positives have surfaced. Make sure that you look for them.

Nancy, who had three daughters, was married for eleven years before she became a single parent. Although she had confidence in her ability to cope with her work and childcare responsibilities, she was soon put to the test. Every night when she returned from work, the first thing she did was begin to make dinner. But Tara, her youngest daughter, seemed to choose that moment to have a tantrum. At first, Nancy got angry with her. Then she challenged herself to find the underlying positives in this situation. She realized that after a long day away from each other, Tara needed her mother more than she needed dinner. Nancy had a talk with her daughters, and they all decided that they'd spend a little time together when they arrived home before beginning other tasks. By finding the positives in the relationship, like how important they were to her, Nancy was able to make a good change for her family.

You can help this process along by acknowledging the many positive things that affect you and your children. Reflect on the fact that you are becoming more secure, have the love and affection of your children and those closest to you, and feel good about what you've learned in getting to this point. And by continuing to focus on the positives, you and your children will become closer and more cohesive as time goes on. Make sure to take a moment to acknowledge these positive experiences that make you feel good about yourself. It's much more important to focus on these than to ruminate on negatives. Try these tips:

- Remember that nothing is permanent. Life is always changing. What happens to us today will be understood differently tomorrow. Keeping this in mind helps you remain flexible so that you don't get stuck.

- It's easy to criticize ourselves or see things in a negative light. Each time a negative thought comes up, try changing it to a positive. For example, instead of saying, "My kids never listen to me," say, " My kids listened to me the last time I asked them to help me."

- Each day, keep a list of the events of the day that made you feel good. Review them at night before you go to sleep and once again in the morning. This will help you keep them in mind and feel better about yourself. Practice this exercise over time. You will find the good feelings stay with you even when things become more difficult.

- Practice recognizing the positive things your children do and say while looking past their negative behaviors. This doesn't mean that you abandon discipline; but when you take your daily break to review positives, remember not to cloud it with intrusive thoughts of negative incidents. The more that you can acknowledge the good things that your children do and the positive feelings that you have about them, the better they feel about themselves and the better you will feel about them.

There are always positives that underlie everything that happens. Take a moment each day to find them.

2. Develop a "Can-Do" Attitude

Our attitudes affect our motivations and actions. Having a "can-do" attitude inoculates us against our disappointments and motivates us to pursue new avenues. We need to have confidence in how resilient we can be. As human beings, we all go through stable periods and times of transition. If we recognize that life is always changing, we are better prepared to face the effect of these changes.

Brad, for example, was a can-do guy. He realized that he couldn't keep his well-paying but high-pressure job with a consulting company when he became a single parent. His boys, ages twelve and fourteen, were too young and vulnerable to be left alone as much as that job required. So Brad took a less important job at commensurately less pay so he could be more available to the boys. It was a difficult transition for him, and he worried about his loss of income. However, he had a good attitude. This enabled him to talk to his boss about some ideas he had that would make money for the company as well as for him. Brad's boss was open to these ideas, and Brad was encouraged that his new arrangements would work out well for everyone involved.

Expectations are a big factor in developing a can-do attitude. If you think about it, "failing" at something often means being disappointed at not meeting your expectations. If this is true, then changing your expectations can lead to success and satisfaction. In order to make this happen, each of us has to be realistic about what we can expect from ourselves and others.

Keep these tips in mind:

- Pay attention to your health. Maintaining a good attitude takes energy, and the healthier we are, the more energetic we feel. Make sure to eat nutritionally and regularly (try not to overeat or eat late at night). Get regular medical checkups. Maintain a consistent sleep schedule (go to sleep at the same time each night) and exercise regularly (just taking a ten-minute walk each day can enhance your energy).

- Be aware of what's important to *you*. You will be more motivated to maintain a good attitude if you know you're accomplishing your goals. And staying aware of what's important will prevent you from becoming distracted by trying to please others. Keeping your values in mind will help.

- Your attitude can influence the choices you make and their outcomes. Fine-tune your attitude toward events and people. Say "sometimes" or "often" instead of "always." Be specific ("I missed that opportunity") instead of global ("I'm a failure"). Take ownership of what you have control over ("I didn't prepare enough") instead of blaming ("That was unfair"). Remove the word "should" from your vocabulary. Be assertive. Rather than say, "I should have," say, "It's important to me that . . ."

- Develop methods that relieve you of stress and help you to *let go*. Everyone needs a break; taking time for yourself helps you rededicate yourself to the task at hand. Create a quiet time for yourself each day (just a few minutes will do) to put aside all outside distractions. Try not to think about anything during this time and practice a relaxation method, meditation, or prayer.

- Get involved in a weekly activity that has nothing to do with your family or job (participate in a sport, join a social group, or volunteer your time).

- Plan and manage your time. You will be more efficient and have more energy for emotional issues. Keep your important and positive life choices in mind and stay consistent to your values.

Practicing a can-do attitude makes a big difference.

3. Keep Your Strengths in Mind

When we face adverse situations and change, we often forget our past accomplishments and successes. Just by living our lives, we have all developed many life skills, and it's important to call on them when we need to. At the same time, we need to remember that no parent, in any type of family, possesses all the skills he or she needs in order to be successful all the time. Once we accept this, we can call upon what we do know to help us find the answers to our questions.

Dave's story exemplifies this point. After his separation from his wife, he became the primary caregiver for his children. Up until that time, he had not spent a lot of time providing childcare. But he didn't let that stop him. He realized that as a manager of a group in his company he knew how to organize people to get things done. Approaching his task at home as he would at work, he first reviewed the territory. He read a few parenting books, talked to some people whose knowledge about children he trusted, and organized a family meeting to get input from and earn the cooperation of his children. With all this information, he was able to begin his new role as single parent with confidence and with his resources martialled.

It's helpful to remember that we are already programmed to solve problems and find alternatives so that we can accomplish what we want. Keeping our strengths in mind when we face new situations and problems helps us reach our goals. Here are two great ways to keep your strengths in mind. First, try to have patience; trust that with time and thoughtfulness, you will find answers. And second, recall your past successes.

You can use this second strategy in stages. First, sit back and relax. Let your mind go back to an experience about which you felt successful and proud of yourself. It doesn't matter if the achievement was trivial or minor, just that you felt it was successful. Now open yourself up to the feelings you had when you realized you had a success. Stay with those feelings. Let them get deep inside your body and resonate throughout.

Now, think of the skills you used to accomplish this success. Write them down.

Do this once a week and you'll see how readily you can use these strengths that you have acknowledged.

Here are some possibilities of strengths for your list:

- I'm patient.
- I like people.
- I'm flexible.
- I am responsible.
- I'm affectionate.
- I'm independent.
- I can organize things.
- I'm a planner.
- I'm good natured.
- People like me.
- I'm a good communicator.
- I have a good sense of humor.
- I have a good memory
- I'm a great cook.
- I have good insight.
- I'm a hard worker.

There's one important strength to add to your list if it's not already there: *I know where to turn—to people or other resources—when I don't have the answers.* Then you can incorporate what you learn from these sources as a new skill.

Keeping your strengths in mind helps you stay on track. It's useful to keep your list on hand and review it each day. When you face a problem, it's your strengths that help you find a successful outcome.

4. Meet Your Children's Needs

Among all the important things in your life, there is nothing more important than meeting the needs of your children. You naturally spend a lot of time doing things for them: keeping a home, feeding them, watching over them, helping them with their school work, driving them to and from activities. Essentially, you are involved in every aspect of their lives. But what *do* children really need? How can you tell if you're meeting all their needs?

Allison asked herself these questions after her divorce when she found herself very concerned about how her children were coping. Because she had to work longer hours, her mother helped with childcare. Their father wasn't visiting much, and the kids often asked about him. She also noticed that there had been some regression in her children's schoolwork.

Allison decided that she needed to talk to each of her children to share her concerns, ask them how they felt, and ask them what they felt they needed. Matt, age five, tried to reassure her that everything was okay. She said, "I'm glad that you are concerned about my feelings and that you feel that everything's okay." Samantha, age nine, got very upset and cried. Allison took her daughter in her arms and said, "You're really upset. I know that this has been a hard time for you." Then she said, "I'm proud of you both that you've tried to help out so much. That pleases me."

Together, the three of them came up with a new plan. They decided that when Allison was at work, she would call the children at specified times to say hello. They would arrange a block of time one morning or afternoon on the weekend that they would call "family time," and they'd each have a turn deciding how to spend that time together. They also decided that each child would have a special time, once a week, alone with Mom.

Allison also talked about her concerns regarding school and encouraged the kids to put more effort into their studies. "I have confidence in you and would like to work together with you on this," she said. "I would like to hear about school each day after dinner and help you with your school work." Matt and Samantha both agreed.

Finally she suggested that she help both children write a letter to their father once a week in which they could let him know what they'd been up to. Although they were anxious about this, they were glad that Allison offered to help.

Let's look at Allison's approach to meeting her children's needs.

- She shared the problem with them.
- She acknowledged their feelings.
- She acknowledged her own feelings.
- She reinforced them positively by telling them the things she appreciated.
- Then she shared her thoughts on how they could work together to improve things in order to secure their cooperation.
- She also recognized that the best approach was to look at the environment as a whole and to structure activities that create consistency for the whole family.

Instead of trying to solve the problem for her children, she brought them into the loop and enlisted their participation. She also maintained her leadership role in the family by suggesting a structure for change and respectfully guiding the children to participate. This created the security and cooperation so important in single-parent families.

Allison is a good model to follow because she approached her children with respect and incorporated their resources in meeting their needs and hers.

5. Take Good Care of Yourself

It's easy to forget your own needs, yet you are very important. As a single parent, your whole family is dependent on your leadership, management, and coping skills. But precisely because you spend so much effort and time meeting the needs of your children, you can end up having no time for yourself. Or, if you do take some time or spend money on something you want, you can end up feeling guilty or selfish.

If this is the case, then you need to evaluate your own needs, keeping in mind that you are as important as anyone else in your family. If you can satisfy your own needs, you will have a great deal more energy and strength to be the parent you want to be.

When you evaluate your goals, keep in mind that these change over time. Many parents derive great satisfaction and fulfillment from caring for their children when they are young. However, as children grow, their needs change: they need to develop good peer relationships, and learn to be independent and self-sufficient. As they mature in this way, it's important for you to find ways to meet your needs outside of your relationship with them. Instead of feeling guilty when you pursue other interests and take time for yourself, remind yourself that you're doing what's healthy for your children.

Consider Nate, a single father who, after his divorce, devoted so much time to caring for his three boys that he lost touch with most of his friends. Because the rest of his family lived a day's drive away, his only adult relationships were with coworkers, whom he saw irregularly at best. Though Nate loved his children, he found himself growing resentful over all his household responsibilities and realized that he needed time away. He contacted his oldest friend and suggested that they meet for a few beers. Though he worried about finding someone to stay with the children, it wasn't hard—he called another parent he knew and got the name of a teenager who had been babysitting for several years. Nate and his friend enjoyed each other's company so much that they decided to meet every couple of weeks to shoot baskets, and get a bite to eat. As it turned out, they eventually joined a basketball league and their team fell into the habit of going out together after the games. In fact, one of the guys had a sister whom he introduced to Nate. They hit it off. Soon, Nate was making dates not just for beer and basketball, but to take his new friend out to dinner and a movie. And much to his surprise, his children seemed less irritable and more cooperative around the house—a bonus he hadn't counted on.

Here's how you can meet your needs, as Nate did.

- Maintain good friendships.
- Find an activity that you enjoy and participate in it regularly.
- Together with the children, develop a timetable at home so that everyone gets to enjoy time alone.
- Seek out activities designed to let children be with other children while adults mingle with other adults. Religious organizations and groups such as Parents without Partners regularly schedule such activities.
- Developing a hobby can be particularly satisfying.

Take your own needs seriously. Rather than just settling, find ways to enhance your enjoyment and satisfaction. Remember, you don't have to sacrifice yourself for your children. The more that you can integrate meeting your needs along with the needs of your children, the more satisfied everyone will be.

6. Learn to Juggle

As a single parent, you have many responsibilities. Ultimately, everything is up to you. Even if you're lucky enough to have good friends and family members who support you, no one can relieve you of your primary responsibilities to your children. No matter how well you try to plan your time so that everyone's needs are attended to, something else always comes up unexpectedly.

We talk about "balancing" our responsibilities but in truth, there's no real balancing. It's obvious that some responsibilities are always more important than others; for example, securing the welfare of your children and keeping a good job certainly head the list. But other priorities change from day to day. Quite likely, it's the unexpected that becomes your first priority.

To maintain a healthy perspective on all you have to accomplish, it's best to:

- Realize that you can't do it all
- Prioritize your tasks, as best you can
- Learn to manage your time more efficiently.

Sally recently discovered this for herself. She read somewhere that 20 percent of what we do produces 80 percent of the reward. So she decided to make a list of her daily activities and prioritize them. She gave "1" to her most important tasks and "10" to the least important. Then for a week, she decided that every day she would make sure to complete only those activities to which she'd assigned a 1 or 2 and then do as many of the others as she could afterward. When she reviewed her accomplishments for that week, she felt good about what she'd accomplished. She was also relieved to realize that she didn't regret the items that she was not able to complete. She decided that she would plan each week this way.

One way to assess how you use your time is to record the activities you do each day for a week. At the end of the week, review each item on the list and prioritize them: give a 1 to necessary activities, 2 to optional activities, and 3 to activities that are unnecessary. Then sketch out a day-by-day plan for the upcoming week, recording the necessary activities before the optional ones (remember to include time for fun and relaxation). After a week, evaluate your success in managing responsibilities.

Here are some points to keep in mind:

- Planning each week's activities saves time.

- Schedule to do your priority activities during those certain times each day when you have more energy and motivation.

- Learn to say "no" when it's appropriate; you'll be able to accomplish more than you think.

- Take regular breaks during the day, and schedule in quiet times; this will give you more energy.

- Vary scheduled activities to keep you interested and motivated. For example, take a pleasurable walk after doing the weekly laundry.

- Keep your priorities in mind, especially when something unexpected comes up.

Keeping your priorities clear and knowing when to say no will help you get more done and have more fun doing it, both alone and with your children.

7. Share the Load: You Can't Do Everything

As your responsibilities for your family and job pile up, it's easy to begin to feel as if you're responsible for everything. It becomes increasingly difficult to let any task go. This begins a vicious cycle: you feel as if you have to do everything yourself because you can't trust anyone else to do it. And then you begin to accomplish less and less, which makes you feel as if you have more and more to do—and only *you* can do it.

Learning to let go and accept that you can't do everything will help you accomplish much more, as Tom found out. He had trouble letting go. His kids were so important to him that he believed he had to care for them entirely by himself. Aside from his job, his whole life focused on his children. And because he proved himself so conscientious, everyone counted on him. Soon he was even taking care of his children's friends because, he reasoned, this would benefit his children, too.

But gradually he began to have less energy and feel more depressed. He also began making his children promises that he couldn't keep. Disappointed and angry with himself, he became irritable and critical of his children. One day, after a bad fight, his youngest child tearfully blurted out, "You're always so grumpy and mad at us."

To his credit, Tom knew she was right and vowed to change. The first thing he did was remind himself that there was no way he could do it all. Each day he wrote on his calendar, "I can't do it all." At the end of the day he asked himself, "What can I let go of tomorrow?" He made sure to let go of at least one thing. He stopped taking work home one day each week. He called the parents of his children's friends and arranged carpools to activities so that he wouldn't be the sole driver. And he asked family members to spend some weekends with his kids so that he could have some time to himself. Because he let go gradually and in such a responsible way, he didn't feel guilty about it. And to his delight and surprise, he discovered that his children were becoming increasingly independent and responsible as well. They were even helping out more around the house, often without having to be asked. As a result, they were all enjoying each other much more.

Letting go can be tough. Here are some strategies to try:

- Remind yourself each day that you can't do everything, and that it's not stress that gets you down, but *distress*.

- Take a fifteen-minute to a half-hour break once or preferably twice a day and practice a relaxation exercise such as meditation, progressive relaxation, guided imagery, yoga, or regulating breathing—whichever is most comfortable for you.

- Pay attention to those times when you are the most distressed, and try to eliminate or change those instances. For example, you may experience great distress over the responsibility of preparing dinner each night. Though you can't eliminate having dinner, you can think of creative solutions: cook dinner every other night and treat your family to take-out on alternating nights.

- Prioritize your important responsibilities and do them first.

- Put aside a time for fun just for you each week. Even a short interval can be refreshing if you take advantage of it on a regular basis.

Letting go is an important skill to develop. If you practice consistently, you'll be surprised at how much easier it will become.

8. Decisions: A Family Affair

Once you accept that you can't do everything, you begin to recognize how helpful sharing decisions can be. You also start to realize how many people are available to you to help.

Sharing decision making with your children is particularly gratifying because it not only lightens your load but also teaches them responsibility. If you're in good contact with your kids' other parent (a subject that is addressed in another chapter), sharing decision-making about the major aspects of your children's lives, such as school, discipline, and activities outside the home, makes children feel very secure. Collaborating on decision making with those in whose care you leave your children, whether babysitters, daycare providers, or family members, makes transitions smoother and stabilizes the quality of the care your children receive.

The more that you can share making decisions with your children, the better your household will run and the happier everyone will be. When you include the children in making family decisions, they feel important, as if they are part of the process. Think about it: when someone tells you to do something, you often feel defensive and controlled, which makes you less likely or willing to cooperate. On the other hand, if someone says, "I think that this would be the best solution to the problem. What do you think?" you would be more invested in the eventual outcome. When children are approached in this way, they feel acknowledged and respected. An added benefit is that this positive attitude gets transferred to other aspects of your relationship with them.

For instance, when Charlotte wants to make a decision, she approaches her children in the following way. "I'm not happy with the way bedtimes are working out. I'm concerned that we haven't agreed on our structure and rules about getting to bed, and it would make me feel good to have your input so that we can make a mutual decision."

By addressing the problem this way, Charlotte takes "ownership" of her feelings. (She does this by saying she's "concerned" and that she would "feel good.") She lets her children know what is motivating her to speak up—that she wants their input and values a mutual decision. This disclosure is the first step.

Now she is ready to assert her leadership position. "I was thinking that we could begin the bedtime process at seven o'clock by turning the TV off. I thought that because Ben is the oldest, he would have a bedtime of 8:30 and Jen of 8 o'clock. What do you think?" When the children respond, she genuinely considers their ideas. Ben says that seven o'clock is too early as his favorite TV show finishes at eight. Charlotte asks Jen what she thinks and Jen agrees. "I understand," Charlotte says, "but I'm concerned that if we do that, you both will get to bed too late." Now they are beginning to collaborate. Eventually they agree to turn the TV off at eight o'clock, and to make bedtimes at 8:15 and 8:45. They also agree to Charlotte's idea that the children change into their pajamas before the TV show begins. With this kind of shared decision making, the likelihood of success is much greater than if Charlotte had come up with the plan herself.

It's important to show respect for each person included in making decisions. Hear them out. Acknowledge their feelings. And don't forget to assert what's important to you by stating your feelings ("I'm concerned about you getting to bed too late").

9. Build a Support Network

Every parent needs a support network, and for single parents, it's particularly important. Networks are not only an antidote to the isolation many single parents experience, but also a means of survival. When you have a support network, it's easier to ask for help when you need it because the structure is already in place. And you're less likely to feel inadequate and guilty asking for help when you know that the support is reciprocal. Just knowing that you can trust the support that you have developed gives you confidence in yourself and what you can accomplish.

What many of us don't realize is that networks need constant nurturing and rebuilding. The most resilient networks are those that are composed of a variety of resources. In this way, you don't become overly dependent on any one member.

Sometimes, taking the first step to creating such a network is the hardest task of all, as Kathy realized. She was feeling very unhappy because all her energy went into taking care of her daughter, the house, and her job: she had nothing left over for herself. Bev, one of her coworkers who was also a single parent, noticed how unhappy she was and invited Kathy to join her single parent support group. Kathy was reluctant. She felt insecure, and she also wasn't sure that she could find someone to watch her daughter while she was out. But Bev's teenage daughter volunteered to babysit, and Kathy found that she loved the group. What a relief it was to realize that she wasn't alone—that other single parents felt exactly as she did! She also met some very nice people and was eager to know them better. From this modest beginning she was able to construct a support network on which she came increasingly to depend.

To create a support network yourself:

1. First assess your existing network. Draw up a list of every person that you know who is or has been a part of your life. Include those people with whom

you've not been in touch for some time and those with whom your relationships may be less well defined.

2. Identify who is part of your present support system and who is not. Of those not included, consider those you could eventually include.

3. Organize your list into the following categories: who is most available, who you would like to be available, who is closest to you emotionally, and who would come through in a pinch. You may be able to think of other categories to include as well.

4. Now divide your list into functional support categories: who can you turn to for emotional support, childcare, help with transportation, economic help, social companionship, and/or spiritual guidance? Families that have children the same ages as yours could provide a social network for all of you.

5. Finally, consider whom you might have left out and if it would be worthwhile to nurture these relationships so that they could be included.

6. Once you have completed and organized this list, review it periodically for any changes you would like to make. This will be very helpful to you as needs arise.

You can look for support at your church, synagogue or mosque; through self-help groups, internet websites, and/or chat rooms for single parents; your children's school, the information and referral services of your local government; and through a therapist who has expertise in working with single-parent families.

Once you are open to it, there is plenty of support around you. Keep in mind that support is a two-way street. You will feel strengthened by helping others, and vice versa.

10. Involve the Other Parent

If you're one of the readers who is a single parent through divorce, you'll probably recognize that, though you've lost a spouse, your children haven't lost a parent. No matter how hurt or angry you are, you still have to deal with your ex. This involvement will last as long as you have children in common.

Divorce also breaks one family into three: yours, the one your children share with the other parent, and the one that they share with you and the other parent (the "divorced family"). The more you and your former spouse can work together on behalf of your children to make all three families work well, the better they will feel.

You will work together better if you remember that:

- **He or she loves the kids, too.** Your former spouse loves your children and cares about their welfare as much as you do. Remembering this will help you through many of the disagreements that may arise. You probably won't see eye-to-eye about many issues, but acknowledging that the other person's intentions arise from love, as yours do, will sow the seeds of a more cooperative relationship.

- **Children feel loyalty to both of you.** They may not want to talk about their feelings about the other parent, but they will always want you to support them in their relationship with the other parent. If you say negative things about the other parent, your children will end up feeling anxious and torn. When children talk to you about their relationship with your former partner, listen empathetically, but reinforce the fact that they are responsible for their relationship with the other parent, not you.

- **Be consistent on the rules.** When you collaborate on rules with your former spouse, your children will benefit. Create rules and expectations for the children that are consistent between households; this makes children less anxious because they have to make fewer adjustments. If you can't collaborate in this way, then make sure that the rules in each household are clear to everyone, and respect the other parent's authority when your children are with him or her.

- **Be patient during transitions.** Transitions are particularly stressful. Moving from one household to another takes an emotional toll on children: some become withdrawn, some overly demanding. It's important to try to be patient with them during these times. Accept that this is their way of coping with stress. You can ease the transition by creating consistent routines. Whether it's having a particular treat waiting each time they return home or allowing them an hour each to do their own things before getting back into the routine of your household, regular events and activities will smooth the transition.

- **Try to "double up."** Children appreciate both parents' involvement in their lives. They appreciate both the attention and the knowledge that two parents are looking out for them. When both parents keep in touch with their children's school progress, attend school plays and sport events, and oversee other extracurricular activities, kids feel more secure and derive more satisfaction. Try to organize your children's activities with the other parent so that both your schedules can be accommodated. If nothing works, you may have to take turns attending activities. If you stick to this regimen consistently, your children will adjust to it.

All of these suggestions will help bridge the gap between the three families your children belong to. Respecting the involvement and concern of the other parent improves everybody's life.

11. Develop Rituals and Traditions

Traditions, which generally exist across generations, are different from routines in that they create in us a sense of continuity that embraces the past and anticipates the future. Traditions can tie us together even though we may be physically apart. For example, if your children are not with you on Valentine's Day, you might call them or send them a card to express your love for them. Traditions also create opportunities for extended family get-togethers that contribute to your sense of security and support.

If your family is in the midst of great change, then developing new rituals, routines, and traditions is especially important to maintain a sense of cohesiveness and stability. To create new rituals and routines for your single-parent family, begin by drawing upon those that were part of your extended family: if they worked in the past, they will probably still work. Your children will appreciate the continuity and have a better sense of mastery over their own lives.

When you and your children collaborate to maintain these routines and traditions, it reduces the opportunities for conflict. Daily life also runs more smoothly. It's helpful if you're in contact with your children's other parent, to see to it that holidays and important events are arranged cooperatively so that your children can look forward to these occasions. Your children will feel more secure and remember these times with fondness.

When Jim split up with his wife, he had to pick up his children from day care, bring them home, and make dinner—he could no longer play with them while his wife made dinner. He tried to make up for it by spending the extra time with both children to read to them before bed. Though they at first missed playtime with Dad before dinner, they now look forward to this special time with him at bedtime.

Jim also paid careful attention to all the routines that his children had enjoyed before the separation. He discussed with his children which ones they could still observe—like participating in church activities—and which would have to change. They also decided to spend the important holidays at home with just the three of them after his children expressed a desire for this. After a period of trial and error around scheduling, both he and the children felt comfortable with the new rhythm of their lives.

Keep the following in mind:

- Even the most mundane daily event can become special—Friday night pizza, Sunday morning French toast, the Saturday morning walk to get the newspaper.
- Observe as many of your family's former routines as you can.
- If you have to make changes, get input from your children.
- Be realistic about what routines to keep, which to change, and which to discard.
- Maintain a good balance. Share some rituals with others (your extended family, other single-parent families, for instance), but keep some exclusively for yourselves.
- Pay special attention to holidays—they are highly emotional times and you need to consider what will satisfy all of you.

The holidays, routines, and rituals we observe will be the legacy we leave for our children.

12. Learn to Manage Your Stress

Stress is an inevitable part of living. We tend to think of it in a negative light, but without some stress we wouldn't be stimulated or motivated to do anything. Stress is your body's reaction to any change in equilibrium. It has a physiological as well as a psychological component. Physically, your body secretes chemicals that prepare you to cope with whatever you are encountering; this is called "adaptive energy."

When you allow stress to overtake you, however, your body and your mind are less able to adapt. The danger, therefore, is in over-reacting to your stress. With all that you have to think about and do, it's easy for this to happen. That's why managing your stress is important. The security and stability of your family depends on your strength, adaptability, and resilience.

The first step in managing your stress is to assess how you are handling it now. Answering these questions can help you evaluate how you react to stress:

- Are you easily frustrated and quick to react?
- Are you more impatient than you were a few years ago?
- Does a change in your schedule overwhelm you?
- Do you feel like you can never relax?
- Do you find that your children and colleagues are reacting more defensively to you?
- Are you concerned about your eating habits or having trouble sleeping?

If you answered "yes" to many of the above questions, it's likely that you're overly stressed, and it's important to find a means of stress management that works for you. But before getting into specifics, try to maintain a positive attitude even though you feel stressed. Having a positive perspective opens you up to other possibilities and solutions.

There are many specific stress-management techniques, and it's best to find the one that suits your lifestyle and temperament. Many people manage their stress by:

- Exercising regularly and vigorously
- Eating well to stay healthy
- Learning meditation and relaxation techniques
- Staying flexible in the face of change
- Knowing their own strengths and limitations, and asking for help when needed
- Learning time-management strategies
- Setting aside time for fun

Randy discovered support groups after her divorce. In one group, she was given a progressive relaxation tape that guided her in tightening and then relaxing every muscle group: this eases tension in your whole body. Randy listened to the tape each night for a month and was very pleased with how much more relaxed she was. It also helped her concentrate on what was really important to her. This tape became a staple of her stress-management program.

Randy also found that planning her time well helped her feel less anxious about getting things done. By more carefully managing her time, she found more space for herself. Realizing how important this was, she helped her children schedule time for themselves as well, and time for her to spend privately with each child. By paying attention to her schedule, she created more time for herself and her family and reduced her anxiety along the way.

Take advantage of the many resources—in bookstores, parent centers, and online—to help you. Getting a handle on stress will help your children and your family life in countless ways.

Once your stress is more under control, become proactive. That is, maintain your stress at a manageable level so that it doesn't reach crisis proportions again.

Part II
Talking and Listening

13. Show Respect

Respect is at the core of every meaningful and close relationship and a part of every meaningful conversation. To respect another person is to genuinely accept and value the importance of that person in your life. We learn to respect others when we ourselves feel respected. It's like a circle: respect develops from being respected. In a respectful relationship, each person feels open to the influence of the other.

We can show respect in subtle ways—even in nonverbal ways—during every important conversation we have. Think about how you greet your daughter when she comes home from school. From experience, you know that she's tired by the end of the day and is looking forward to her snack. If the first thing you say is, "How was your day?" then you're paying attention to your need for information and not respecting her emotional and physical needs for quiet and something to eat. It's much more respectful to say, "I'm glad to see you. Here's some milk and cookies." This way, she will feel acknowledged and appreciated and will be open to receive your efforts.

Showing respect also means having expectations for others and trusting that they have the capacity to meet the expectations. Because Bill feels guilty about the effects of the divorce on his children, he tends to lessen his expectations of them. If he comes home from work, for example, and the chores he asked them to do aren't done, he gets mad—but then he ends up doing the chores himself. Chuck, on the other hand, respects that the children can be responsible for doing chores to help out. When the chores are not done, he takes the time to talk with them about the importance of chores. He has also worked out a system of rewards and consequences to help his children learn responsibility. Furthermore, Chuck reciprocates by making sure to follow through on his children's expectations of him as their father. Of course, being realistic about expectations is really important.

Talking about your expectations in a manner that shows respect is essential to the quality of the relationship. Saying, "It's important to me that you get your homework done" shows respect; saying, "You'd better get your homework done," is a demand.

Remember: even if you are upset with your children, their feelings are just as important (to them) as yours are (to you).

Do you take these actions to show respect?

- I take the other person's perspective into consideration.
- I try to understand the other person's point of view.
- I try to speak from my point of view and opinion rather than think that the other person is just "wrong."
- I include my feelings when I talk to others.
- I don't criticize others when I'm talking to them.
- I try to focus on the positives when I'm talking.

After each significant conversation, review it in your mind. Remember what you said that helped the other person to feel respected and what that person said to you that indicated respect. Pay attention to how good you feel because respect was communicated. If you can't remember anything, then think of something that you each could have said that would have communicated respect. You may want to keep a notebook of these reflections. That way, you can review them at the end of the day or week.

Remember, having expectations of others and meeting their expectations shows respect. By being respectful, we create relationships that are trusting, caring, secure, and close.

14. Make Time to Talk

Talking often gets taken for granted in family life. We assume that we talk to each other all the time. But if you stop and think about it, much of what passes for conversation isn't really a thoughtful exchange of ideas.

Often, we communicate with each other when we want something from another person, or when we are angry, anxious, or upset. When we're in this frame of mind, much of what we say comes out sounding like a threat or a demand.

Because everyone is so busy these days, we also tend to talk to each other on the run. When this happens, it's likely that the other person isn't really paying attention, but is distracted by their own needs. In these cases, we receive hurried replies that make us feel ignored and unimportant.

What's even worse, though, is when we don't talk at all, but keep things inside. This creates walls between people. Over time, as the walls get thicker and harder to tear down, intimacy suffers. When my children were young, for example, I worked at two jobs and went to school. I'd come home for dinner, but return to the office and not come back until they were asleep. One night, I happened to get home about eight o'clock, only to have one of my sons look up from his homework and say to me, "What are you doing here, Dad?"

After that wake-up call, I put aside one evening a week to spend with my family and dedicated Saturday mornings to my three sons. We'd spend time as a foursome, and I'd spend one-on-one time with each boy as well. We all felt good about this.

This experience proved to me that we can't just expect that we'll find the time to talk with each other in satisfying and close ways. *We have to make the time happen.*

Here are some ideas that can help you find time to be together:

- Call a family meeting to talk about family conversation. In advance of the meeting, ask everyone in the family to write down his or her time commitments for the month. (If you have young children, ask them to dictate their schedule and have someone write it down for them.) Buy or make a big calendar and bring it to the meeting.
- Ask one person to serve as secretary. This person collects everyone's schedules and enters them onto the master calendar.
- Meet at the appointed time to talk about spending time together. Make sure to set aside times for the whole family to be together and for you and each of your children to be together.
- Write these scheduled times on the master calendar and display it prominently in a room used by all members of the family.

There will be times when something important comes up and one or more family members won't be able to keep their commitments. In these cases, scheduling "rain check" dates is helpful. It's also important to talk with each other about ways to handle those times that you can't make up.

Becoming aware of the need for meaningful conversation—taking the time to listen to each other and making the time to talk when you have important things to say—will help everyone in the family feel more valued and respected. It will also foster family cohesiveness.

15. Pay Attention to Feelings

Feelings motivate our actions and thoughts. In many of our conversations, especially with people close to us, what we really want to talk about is how we feel—not specific details—and how the other person feels. Sometimes we have feelings we don't recognize or don't pay attention to. Yet our feelings are always there, even if they're out of our awareness. They define us as human and allow us to experience life as we know it.

Yet many people find it hard to talk about feelings. They think of feelings in a negative light. They worry about becoming "too emotional," and appearing too vulnerable. Yet when we openly accept our feelings and get comfortable expressing them, our relationships become much more intimate. We are at our best when we share our feelings.

Another problem many people have is that they have trouble finding the right words to say what they really mean. Sonia, for example, rarely says what's on her mind. When someone gives her something she likes, such as a compliment or a gift, she says, "Oh you shouldn't have done that!" when what she really means to say is, "That makes me feel good." When she wants her children to know how upset she is, she says, "What a mess!" instead of, "I'm angry that you did that." As a result, the people Sonia talks to often leave conversations with her feeling unsatisfied.

That's why it's important to learn to use "feeling words," such as, "I feel sad when . . ." or "I feel good when . . ." in our conversations. When we become fluent in using feeling words, we are better able to recognize and understand our experience and the experience of others. As a result, we have more of a sense of control over ourselves and more insight into others.

Here are some ways you can begin to focus on your emotional awareness.

When you're talking with someone close to you, listen to see how many times you say a feeling word when you are talking. Also listen to see how many times the other person uses a feeling word.

Practice recognizing the feelings that you have when you are talking. Start by asking yourself whether you feel good or bad about what you are saying. Then think of other feeling words that you could use in place of "good" or "bad."

Practice recognizing the other person's feelings. How does she express happiness or sadness? Are her feelings reflected in her face? In his tone of voice? In his posture? In the words he uses?

Be sure you include your feelings when you are talking.

Try this game at a family meeting. Have each person name a feeling word. Then go around again and again, naming feeling words until no one can name a feeling word. Give a prize to the last person standing. Write all the words down, make copies, and give a copy to each family member.

Feelings are complicated, and it's important that we respect how powerful they can be. Here are some key things to keep in mind.

- Our feelings motivate us to say and do the things that we do.

- Use feeling words to help you say what you mean and to help the other person understand you better.

- Listen for the feelings of others to really understand them.

- Letting other people know you understand their feelings makes them feel good and trust you more.

16. Know Yourself

The way we think and feel about ourselves affects everything we do in life, including how satisfied and fulfilled we feel. It also influences our relationships with others, especially those who are important to us.

Knowing yourself also helps you take responsibility for your actions. The more you know yourself, the more open, assertive, and responsible you can be. At the same time, others are better able to understand you and meet your needs. With self-knowledge, you are more likely to feel satisfied with yourself and others—and closer to them as well. You can ask for help when you need it. This awareness, that no one person can do or know everything, allows you to reach out to others and connect with them in order to share your strengths.

Helping children to know themselves is one of a parent's main goals. But before you can help your children gain self-knowledge, you need to know yourself. To do this, you need to reflect on how your feelings affect you and what is important to you. Being able to recognize your strengths and weaknesses helps you be realistic about yourself and guides you to make choices that are in your best interest.

Take Phil, who felt very frustrated with his ex-wife. She never brought the kids home at the time she was supposed to, which made him very angry. In turn, he had to struggle to contain his negative feelings, which added to his frustration. To resolve his problem, he tried to honestly assess his feelings. He recognized how much he valued his children's feelings. Their need to see their mother took precedence over his frustration with his ex-wife. That helped him cope with this difficulty.

Learning to recognize your true motivations doesn't come easily. One important strategy to use is to take ownership of yourself. This means that you don't blame others or make them responsible for how you feel. Instead, you recognize that you have power over how you feel. So, rather than getting mad at your former spouse and criticizing him, recognize how demeaned you feel and find ways to feel better about yourself (see below).

Another significant action you can take is to keep your feelings in mind. At several intervals during the day, try to:

1. Take a minute and relax.

2. Check how you are feeling about yourself at that moment.

3. Use feeling words to describe your mood. Start with, "I feel good," or "I feel bad." Then try to refine your description using related words such as "pleased," "excited," "frustrated," "angry," "hurt," "concerned," or "worried" to flesh out the depth of your feeling.

4. Check to see if your feelings are related to the moment or to some other aspect of your life.

5. Ask yourself: "Is how I'm feeling consistent with my values and how I value myself?"

6. Consider how you can change your response to be more consistent with your values and feelings.

7. Reward yourself when you are able to act in ways that are consistent with your values and feelings.

8. Practice affirming yourself. One way to do this is to see the positives in each aspect of yourself. For example, instead of describing yourself as "impulsive," you can say that you're someone who likes to quickly size up a situation and take action. Each morning and evening, practice the following statements:
    - I value myself.
    - I am important.
    - I have power over myself.

- My feelings are important.
- I am loved.

Remember, self-knowledge isn't something we're born with: to really know ourselves takes practice and introspection.

Talking and Listening **41**

17. Say What You Mean

Talking with others is harder than it seems. Much of the time, we are in such a hurry to get our point across that we don't take the time to think about what we want to say or say it in a way that others will understand. Instead, we often just blurt out whatever comes to mind, which is rarely what we mean to say. Other times, we aren't in touch with what we mean to say.

As a single parent, it's really important that your children and those close to you understand you and what you want. If they don't, it only adds to your stress and makes life much harder.

When Connie's children return home after a weekend with their father, they are hard to manage. In frustration, she says, "Your father lets you get away with anything." This remark hurts her children's feelings, but even worse, it causes them to have mixed feelings about their father because it underscores the conflict between their parents. Noticing their dismay and hurt, Connie apologizes. She realizes that what she means to say is, "I'm very frustrated when you come home and it's so hard to get you guys in bed."

Talking is the way we discover what our conversations (and relationships) mean. But making our conversations meaningful and satisfying requires attention. Try to:

- Understand yourself and where you're coming from. Ask yourself: "What am I feeling?" and "Why do I want him to know this?"

- Be open, especially with those for whom you care. Openness fosters trust. When people can't be direct with each other, conversations tend to break down. To have open conversations, ask yourself: "Am I comfortable letting her know this?" and "How can I say what I want to so that she will understand and I won't feel sorry that I said it?"

- Be subjective. It's easier to see problems as the other person's fault rather than our own. But when we think this way, we lose the power we have to change the problem. Remember, we all see things from our own point of view, and all we really know is our own feelings. So when we want to say something, it is important to be subjective. That is, be aware that your truth isn't the *only* truth. Talk about what is truly important to you. Accept and respect that the other person might have a different point of view.

- Remember what's positive in the relationship. The more someone means to us, the more we want them to understand us. It's important to acknowledge our importance to each other as much and as often as possible. Remember to say, "I love you," "You're important to me," and "It makes me feel good when you do that," frequently. Encourage your children to do the same.

Try to focus on the positives in your relationship even when you're upset. For example, you can say: "I'm really angry that you didn't finish your chores because of how important it is to me that the bathroom is clean," or "I'm hurt that you are questioning me; I just want you to understand how important it is to me." Saying what you mean takes some thought and practice, but it's well worth it. Remember that the best outcome will be achieved if everyone is open with their feelings and tries to find solutions together.

18. Show Understanding

Perhaps the most important thing you can do in a relationship is to understand the other person. When you feel understood, you feel good; you let your guard down and naturally open up to the other person. Your body relaxes and you feel satisfied. Being understood gets at the core of one's being. Humans have a need to be recognized, and that's what understanding is about.

If we don't get this recognition—if our efforts are ignored or not fully appreciated—we feel hurt, a feeling that registers in our bodies.

Showing understanding goes beyond merely listening, or believing that you understand the other person. It isn't saying, "I understand." And it isn't offering reassurance.

Suppose your son wakes up one morning and says, "Gee, I feel lousy today, and I'm not sure why."

You reply, "You'll feel better tomorrow." It sounds as if you're offering reassurance, but what you're really doing is telling him that he shouldn't feel the way he does. Even if he's just trying to stay home because he has a tough test in school, he will feel discounted. He would feel better if you said, "I'm concerned that you feel bad, but you know our rule that you have to have a fever to stay home." Or, if you know about the test you could say, "I think that you may be worried about the test."

Showing understanding means that you let the other person know that you understand the feeling that motivated their statement. For example:

- When your son gets 100 percent on a science test, he wants you to understand and recognize his *excitement* and *pride*, not ask him what other children got.

- When you show up late for a dinner appointment, your friend wants you to recognize that she's *disappointed*; she doesn't want to hear about the traffic jam that held you up.

In order to do this, you have to take the time and energy to pay attention to the other person. That means shutting out other concerns you may have and focusing on what the person is trying to say.

Following that, it's important to concentrate on the other person's agenda, not your own. Think of it this way: You're on a mission to determine how the other person is feeling, not how *you're* feeling.

Finally, when you think you understand what the other person is saying, then it's essential to give him or her some feedback to show that you have been receptive.

Let's say that your daughter has come home late for dinner, and she looks sad and upset. You could tell her how mad you are that she was late and demand an explanation. That would be an example of paying attention to your own agenda. If, however, you talk to her about how concerned you are that she looks sad and upset, then you are paying attention to her. You're still letting her know that you were worried, but in a way that makes her feel validated. Validation helps people not only feel better but also more relaxed; then, they naturally open themselves up and can be more understanding of you. It's precisely when your daughter feels more relaxed and open that you can ask her why she was late. In other words, address her feelings first; then find out information. When both people show understanding, we feel closer and our relationship is better.

It's easy to express our own feelings first. However, the more understanding you show to others, the more you will be understood.

19. Learn to Actively Listen

Listening sounds easy, as if we don't have to "do" anything. But it doesn't really work that way. Keith, for example, prided himself on being a good listener. He quickly understood what people told him and thought he was being reassuring and helpful when he said things like, "Everything will be all right," or "Here's what you should do ..." But not that many people confided in Keith after a while.

If someone is feeling bad, telling them that things will turn out fine won't help. What they want to know is that you understand their feelings. Similarly, telling someone what to do isn't helpful because that person probably wants to solve the problem themselves. All they want in the conversation is a sympathetic ear. And that's exactly what Keith didn't supply.

In short, there's a big difference between passive "hearing" and active "listening." When we truly listen, we try to understand not only what a person is saying but also what he or she is trying to say and why.

You can become an active listener by learning the principles of active listening.

- *Start from the other person's perspective.* Put yourself in their shoes. View things as they would; try to experience the situation as if you were them.

- *Recognize that the most important part of the message is how the other person feels, not the content of what they say.* For most of us, how we feel defines who we are. Feelings are crucial to identity. When we talk, it's our feelings that motivate us to say what we're saying.

- *Accept the other person's feelings as valid no matter whether you agree or disagree with what is being said.* All feelings are valid. Once you accept this fact, then you are free to deal with content issues; that is, to decide whether you agree or disagree with what the other person is saying.

- *Acknowledge your understanding and acceptance of the other person's thoughts and feelings while avoiding judgement and criticism.* The person to whom you are speaking wants you to recognize what motivated them to initiate the conversation and its importance to them. When you acknowledge this need, they feel understood and validated.

    Say that your mother comes to watch your children while you work and says, "Remember, your children need you to be home for dinner." Now, this can be heard as an antagonistic comment. After all, she's presuming to tell you something you already know. If you're an active listener, you can say, "I appreciate that you are concerned about us." By responding this way, you're recognizing that your mother is trying to be helpful. This will not only help avert a fight, but will leave her feeling as if you heard what she was trying to say.

- *Hold back from responding until the previous four steps have been completed.* This helps you take the time to more fully understand the other person.

Finally, here are two things to avoid:

1. *Making judgements.* When we judge other people, we make them feel self-conscious, bad about themselves, and defensive. Hear other people out without thinking, "This person sounds silly," or "This person sounds mean." Have an open mind and suspend making judgments.

2. *Being critical.* Criticism ("What a silly thing to say!" "How could you possibly think that?") hurts. The bad feelings linger well after the specific criticism itself is forgotten.

When we actively listen, we are more open to each other, understand each other and ourselves better, and give ourselves the opportunity to feel more intimate with each other.

20. Talking with Young Chidren

Because of their immaturity, children may not be able to fully express themselves verbally. Children *show* much of what they are thinking, feeling, and how they are being affected by things through their play and behavior. Children use play as a way to understand their world, work out their problems, and find solutions to problems that are hard to grasp or that bother them. It is also a way for them to feel good about themselves, because through play they learn about accomplishment and mastery.

Joining with your child and letting your child lead you in the play activity makes them feel satisfied and secure. They may not need to talk about anything else. If you press him to talk, you will probably both end up feeling frustrated.

It's important to be receptive to what we call *teachable moments*. Be prepared to respond when you perceive that your child is ready and then follow your child's lead. Here's such a moment: Johnny, age three, asks Sam, his dad, "Why do I have to go to day care?" Sam could explain that it's important to be with other children, or that he has to go to work. But instead, he realizes that he first needs to respond to Johnny's feelings. So he says, "You're not happy about going."

Johnny says, "I want to be with you."

"It makes me feel good that you want to be with me," Sam says, going to a positive feeling first. Then, he refers to his own feelings by saying, "That's important to me, too."

Only after he says this does Sam become specific and answer Johnny's question with facts: "It's important to go to day care because I feel better knowing where you are and that you're safe when I'm at work."

This was a teachable moment. Sam paid attention to Johnny's feelings, acknowledged both of their feelings, and offered a reasonable explanation. This demonstrates Sam's respect for his son. As a result, Johnny truly "heard" his father.

Keep the following in mind:

1. Play is how young children go about understanding their world and expressing themselves.

2. Letting a young child lead you in play helps you understand the child better.

3. It may be hard to get a young child to let you know that she understands you. Forcing her to respond may be threatening to her and frustrating for you.

4. Even though children may not seem to be showing you that they understand, they probably do.

5. Keep your comments short and simple. As much as possible, try to phrase things in children's terms, let them know you understand their feelings, and use your feelings when you want to let them know what you want. For example, "You'd like to keep playing, but I'm unhappy that the toys aren't picked up," and "The rule is that toys are put away before dinner."

6. If you want children to understand or do something, you need to be patient. Repeat your request a few times, gently convey through your movements what you want, and try not to act out of your frustration.

7. Try to be consistent and have clear rules and expectations.

Read these seven suggestions over a few times. It takes a little practice to use them consistently. Be patient with yourself—you'll get it after a while.

21. Talking with Adolescents

The media has conditioned us to dread our children's adolescence. Yet it's a natural period of development—a time of transition, of change. Even though it seems as if your teenager is increasingly preoccupied with his peer group (in an effort to develop new social skills and forge his or her own identity), he or she is still interested in your perspective. In fact, research suggests that during the teenage years, parents have a greater influence over their children than their peer group. And how you talk to your teenager during these years is perhaps the most important factor in how he or she negotiates this critical time. Communicating well with teenage children is always important, and particularly so for single parents.

Independence is one important issue that needs to be addressed. As a single parent, you've probably come to rely on your oldest child for help in managing the household and younger children. When children reach adolescence, though, they become increasingly torn between meeting their family responsibilities and fulfilling their own needs, whether it's spending time on their own or socializing with their peers. Many parents naturally feel disappointed or resentful when they perceive their teenagers pulling back from the family. But it's important for you to consider and respect their needs for independence and more social interaction. Being flexible about your expectations will help. You can also try to enlist your younger children to take on more responsibilities. Then you won't be so dependent on your adolescent child and there will be less tension between you.

You can talk to teenagers using the same communication principles and skills as you did when they were younger. But remember that adolescents are undergoing real physiological and psychological changes. They may be moody because of hormonal changes and nothing that you do will seem right. They also tend to be more self-centered during this period. After all, they're facing many changes. At times it may be hard for them to acknowledge your point of view while seeming desperate that you recognize theirs. And much of their attention is on what their peers are doing, not on what's happening at home.

When Bill's daughter Emily turned twelve, she seemed to him like a different person. He'd always been proud of her, especially in the years immediately after his separation from his wife, when Emily seemed unusually understanding. As the oldest child she happily helped out around the house. He knew he could depend on her whenever he needed to. But after her twelfth birthday, she began challenging his every statement and growing more uncooperative by the day. One day, in desperation over the sour turn in their relationship, he asked to talk with her alone. He discovered during this talk that she felt he wasn't listening to her. She acknowledged that she was particularly hurt because of how hard she tried to help at home and how many outside activities she had. She also wanted more of an opportunity to spend time with her friends. He seriously considered her feelings, acknowledged them, and worked out different expectations with her. Then he and Emily discussed what they'd talked about at a family meeting so that the other children felt included.

Bill used these skills to have a successful interaction with Emily:

- He was respectful and understanding.
- He listened actively and paid attention to feelings.
- He didn't judge or criticize.
- He owned his feelings.
- He considered her needs without acting defensively.

Most of all, Bill drew upon the trust and respect that he and his children had built into their relationship.

22. Talking with Those Close to You

Communication is important in every relationship, but every relationship is different. The ways we talk to our boss, friend, clergy, children, parents, customer, waiter, and doctor are as unique as they are. Each relationship has its own rules, context, and nuances, which can make communicating clumsy and difficult. It may seem as if talking to those close to us is easiest of all, but this isn't always true.

The closer you are to someone, the greater your investment in the relationship. In fact, the reason the relationship is so sensitive is because of how close you feel. That's why talking with someone close to you takes special care. You have to be especially thoughtful so that you don't say something hurtful, especially if it's inadvertent.

What we all want from close relationships is the feeling of being wanted and of being important—that our feelings are important. This is what you need to convey when talking to someone close to you—that the other person is important to you and that their feelings matter.

- When Sarah lost her job, her sister, Blanche, said, "Oh, you'll get another one." This only made Sarah feel discounted and defensive. Blanche didn't mean to do this; she wanted to express her concern and let Sarah know how much she believed in her sister. Saying "you'll get another one" was her way of saying, "I can't imagine anyone not wanting to hire you, you're so competent at what you do." What Sarah wanted her to say was, "That's so upsetting," or "I'm concerned."

- After Al gave a speech to his business associates, he confided to his friend Jack that he'd left out an important point. "Doesn't matter," Jack said, "it was a great speech." He meant to be supportive, but Al assumed that Jack hadn't listened to him or taken his regret seriously. If Jack had said, "I liked the speech, it really motivated me," Al would have felt reassured.

- When Tim came home two hours late, he said to his wife as he handed her a bouquet of flowers, "I feel bad that I hurt your feelings." She smiled and felt better almost instantly. If he had said, "The reason I didn't call you was that there was no telephone available," she wouldn't have felt so conciliatory. She wasn't interested in his reasons; she wanted him to address her feelings, which he did.

When you're speaking to someone close to you:

- Always keep in mind that this person is important to you and that you care about them.
- Let that person know often how you feel about them. Say things like, "I feel close to you"; "I feel good every time I'm with you"; "You're important to me"; "I love you." You can never say these caring words too often.
- Honor the trust between you by being open and honest.
- Honor your commitments. It's easy for those close to you to feel unimportant to you when they are disappointed.
- Listen actively first. Then take responsibility for your feelings when you respond. Make sure to acknowledge how important the relationship is to you. And trust that you can repair any damage that occurs by conveying your true feelings.

The principles of constructive talking are the same for most relationships; when talking with someone close, it's even more important that you observe them. And remember, the more you share your feelings with each other, the closer you'll feel.

23. Talking to the Other Parent

This chapter is for those of you who are divorced or separated from your child's other parent. Despite the fact that you are a single parent, both parents are important in your child's life. Parents don't divorce their children and they remain important figures in their children's lives, no matter what the quality of their relationship is or has been. Children benefit from having a good relationship with both parents even when they are no longer living together. Children who have positive, constructive, nurturing relationships with both parents are happier, develop better relationships, and are more ambitious. That's why it's so important for you to learn to talk to your ex-spouse. Children whose separated parents always bicker have a much harder time growing up and recovering from the hurtful effects of this constant hostility.

Whether you're a custodial or noncustodial parent, your parental authority becomes more difficult to establish after the transition. Both your authority and influence over your child become much more dependent on the quality of your relationship and your commitment with them. If either parent pressures your child to take sides, your child will suffer as well as your relationship with him or her. That's why you always have to keep your child's best interest in mind when talking with the other parent.

Charlie usually saw his children every other weekend and two weeks in the summer. He was infuriated when his former wife told him that she had to pick up the children on Saturday instead of Sunday so that they could attend a family party. He was about to object to what he believed was manipulation on her part. However, he recalled how important it was for his daughter to see her cousins. So he said, "I'm concerned about missing time with the kids, but I recognize that Shelly likes to be with her cousins. It would make me feel good to have the children over for dinner on Wednesday to have more time with them." Obviously, things may not always go as smoothly, but this is an example of keeping your child's welfare in mind.

Cynthia encountered a different problem. It was important to her that her children attend church on Sundays. Their father, who had them every other weekend, was very lax about this, which made Cynthia feel very angry and helpless. However, she was afraid that her anger might make the kids feel like they'd have to take sides. So she told their father, "I'm concerned that they aren't attending church on Sunday, and I'd like to discuss this with you to see if we could find a way that they could attend. I'd even be willing to pick them up or drop them off if that would help. That's how concerned I am." His initial reaction wasn't positive, but she stayed in position and continued to try to let him know how important this was to her. Eventually they worked out a compromise: He would drop them off and pick them up at church but would have more time with them before dropping them off at her house.

When talking to the other parent, it's important to:

- Think of your child's interests first.
- Remember that both parents are important.
- Focus your attention on the issue at hand and don't confuse it with other issues.
- Try to be flexible and open to compromise.
- Remember that you don't want to draw your child into a conflict between you two.
- Try to make sure that you acknowledge some understanding of the other parent's perspective.

Most of all, remember that the quality of your child's relationship with both parents has the most influence on her overall well-being.

24. Talking Creates Change

Human beings have a need to communicate with each other. Words help us understand each other and coordinate our actions with each other. Talking helps us convey what's on our minds, how we are feeling, and how important we are to each other. When we don't talk to each other, we feel distant and mistrustful. In the silence, we are left to interpret each other's actions and try to intuit how to relate to each other. Without language, daily interactions would be difficult and clumsy. The more we talk to each other, the more we understand and the better we can work together.

Despite technological advances like e-mail, we still need to talk to each other face-to-face. This seems to forge a closer connection between us than communicating electronically. We need to take the time to talk, share feelings, understand each other, and work things out.

It's especially important to talk when sensitive feelings and issues come up. Ironically, that's the time many of us clam up because we're afraid of hurting someone's feelings or of being hurt ourselves. The problem is that the less we talk, the more we are left to interpret, and that leaves us open to misinterpretation. Another problem is that when we stop talking about what upsets us, we get in the habit of not talking about other things as well. Without our realizing it, we've erected walls that separate us.

Whatever you don't talk about only grows bigger and creates more distance. It's only when we talk together that our understanding changes. That's because you have incorporated new information and different perspectives from which to evaluate it. Relationships always improve when people talk to each other. This is particularly important in close relationships where talking helps you maintain your trust and intimacy.

Don was devoted to his children, Becky and Billy. Even though he saw them only on weekends and for a month in the summer, he felt that they regarded his home as theirs. He grew concerned, however, when he realized that he hadn't seen Becky in what felt like weeks. She'd just entered middle school, and he was concerned about how she was adjusting. Whenever he tried to call, she wasn't home, and she didn't return his calls. As time went on, he grew increasingly concerned, feeling hurt and rejected. After suffering with these thoughts for several weeks more, he asked Becky to have dinner with him. He tried to deal with the fact that he was angry with her for not keeping in touch before they met—he did this by talking about his feelings with some of his friends—so he could avoid being confrontational with her. His strategy worked. When they sat down together, he was able to calmly say, "I've been concerned that I haven't seen you for a while. I was worried that you might be upset with me." Becky was shocked to hear this. She hadn't been angry with him in the least. Instead, she explained, she'd been picked for the lead in the school play and was so busy practicing that she didn't have a free moment. As soon as she said that, Don felt himself relax. They had a good conversation for the rest of the meal and resolved to stay in closer touch with each other in the future.

Remember that the more you talk with each other, the better your relationship can be. It's also important to remember that it's not enough to talk to each other only when we want something, are upset, or need to make plans.

25. Juggle Work and Home

Juggling the demands of work and family is an especially important task for the single parent. Work pressures and stress can strongly influence your mood and how you respond to your children. And there's no other adult around to take some of the pressure off you. If work pressures are making you depressed or anxious at home, you may withdraw or become short-tempered. When you are feeling this way, it's harder to meet the expectations that you have for yourself and your family.

Perhaps the hardest time of the day for single working parents to achieve balance is when everyone first gets home. That's when parents and children realize how much they missed each other during the day; everyone's eager to reconnect. How easy it would be to give in to how tired you are and how much you need some time for yourself, just to cope! But remember—the first contact that you make with each other at the end of the day can determine what happens after that. So it's important to give each other special attention first, before you put your feet up.

Kim, for example, returned to work after her divorce. Her job was demanding, her boss difficult, and her schedule so variable that she often came home late and in a bad mood. As a result, she was impatient with her kids, which caused her to feel guilty. She had to find a better way to cope.

She asked her children for their ideas. They all responded well to her request. Together, they decided that she would call at specified times when they came home from school. Kim also agreed to call them as she was leaving work to come home; that way, Ann, her twelve-year-old daughter, would know it was time to put the dinner Kim had prepared in the microwave. Bill, age ten, agreed to set the table. She also worked out an arrangement with them to reward them for being helpful. Finally, she asked if she could have ten minutes to herself before dinner so that she could switch gears and collect herself, a request her children gladly granted.

Kim's story is a common one. Happily, she found several ingenious ways to balance the competing demands of work and home. Her solution identifies a number of principles for us:

- Be realistic about what and how much can be changed.
- Accept that you are stressed instead of trying to deny it.
- Recognize that your coping is important to everyone in the family.
- Ask your children to work with you; often, they'll be glad to if given the chance.
- Be open with your children about what you are coping with. This helps them support and cooperate with you.
- Try to organize and plan for family needs such as meals and laundry ahead of time as much as you can.
- Establish consistent practices and routines with your family.
- Instead of letting a problem overwhelm you, try to restructure things to relieve the stress.
- When you do feel overwhelmed, it's useful to take a time-out for yourself so you can cope better. That will help everybody.

Juggling work and home isn't easy. Everyone has to find the right recipe for balance. But keeping these nine principles in mind will help you cope.

26. Handle Work Pressures at Home

One of the real challenges facing you as a single parent is learning how to handle pressure at work so that it doesn't spill over into family life. When you are feeling pressured by your boss, an impending deadline, or interoffice politics, you tend to become more distracted at home, which means you are psychologically less available to your children. This, in turn, makes them more stressed and anxious, and family life becomes harder for everyone.

Consider these points about how work functions in our lives:

- Most of us spend about one-third of our entire day at work.
- Work gives us a sense of pride and identity.
- Work adds to the complexity of life and makes life more interesting.
- By working, we are being good role models for our children.
- Working expands our opportunities for success and satisfaction.
- Work encourages us to concentrate and reduces distraction.
- Having many roles in life is good for our physical and emotional health and enables us to have healthy relationships.
- Work opens us up to new experiences, expands our horizons, makes us more flexible, and stimulates us to better evaluate our objectives.

By reminding yourself of all the benefits of work, you have taken the first step toward handling workplace stress at home.

Be realistic about how you handle pressures so you can find the best way for *you* to handle *your* stress. Joe, for example, is a perfectionist. If everything isn't in order, he gets very stressed. John, on the other hand, likes to be involved in many projects at the same time, enjoying the chaos and challenge that goes along with not having everything in place.

Here are some effective strategies for handling work pressures:

- Develop routines that create consistency for you and your family. This is really important around transitions such as waking up, getting off to school or work, returning home, dinnertime, time for homework, chores, and bedtimes.
- Create a list, from "most pressure" to "least pressure," of the responsibilities that pressure you at work and home. Make a self-tailored plan to tackle each one.
- Be open with your children about your pressures and stress. You can say things like, "I'm often really stressed when I get home from work. I'd like it if I could have ten minutes to myself, so I can relax before we begin making dinner."
- Don't use work pressure as an excuse to be critical of your children. Avoid saying things like, "What's wrong with you? Can't you do anything for yourself?"
- Schedule quiet times at home during which you do no work.
- Take breaks in order to keep your strength up.
- When you feel yourself getting stressed, do a relaxation exercise. For example, slow down your breathing, take a breath, hold it, and then slowly let it go. Do this for several minutes.
- Make sure to get regular exercise, eat regularly, and maintain a healthy diet.
- Talk about your pressures at work to good friends, not to your children.

- Pay attention to how much alcohol you drink and/or how much you smoke. Your health, energy, or ability to handle stress could be affected.
- Make sure to do something fun at least once a week.

No matter how much effort you put into handling work pressures, sometimes there is nothing you can do about them. On days like this, let your children know, in age-appropriate ways, how pressured you feel. Ask for their help—children are usually eager to contribute. It makes them feel important and valued. With some good planning on your part, you will all be able to enjoy each other's company when you have regained your equilibrium. Often, the best antidote to a bad day at work is seeing your family work together.

Working and Playing 65

27. We Are a Team

One of the most important ideas in this book is the notion that you can't do it all, and you can't do it alone. It's important to let some tasks go. For others, you need to find ways to enlist the help of your children. You may be surprised to learn how many resources they have and how eager they are to help you.

It helps when everyone thinks of your family as a team. You can even call yourselves the "____ Family Team." Just getting on board with the team idea conveys a collaborative and cooperative atmosphere that permeates the house. By embracing democratic values at home, you let your children know that you consider everyone responsible to help guarantee the success of the family's efforts.

To be a team, every family member has to respect that every other member is important and entitled to have a voice in family decisions. Though you have certain responsibilities and authority as leader of the team, you must respect each team member as well. Don't use your power to abuse and/or undermine your children.

Let's imagine that you get frustrated because of how hard it is to get everyone to bed on time, and on some nights you yell and scream at them. You get so mad that you become aggressive, forcing them into bed and restraining them from leaving their rooms. By doing so, you are in danger of abusing your power. But even worse, you are violating the value that *everyone is entitled to respect*. On top of that, your strategy is backfiring. You're modeling a hostile, conflictual, and unhappy way of relating to each other. No wonder you feel helpless and inadequate.

Eager to try a new approach, you call everyone together and explain how unhappy you are about what happens at bedtime. You suggest that talking about it together will make a difference. In the subsequent discussion, you discover the reasons why your children don't cooperate. They suggest a new approach to bedtime routines. You decide to give it a try—and sure enough, it works.

What you did was build a team. To accomplish this, begin by talking up the idea of teamwork. To get everyone on board, you can say something like, "You know guys, I was thinking that we'd all feel so much better if we acted more like a team. After all, I can't do everything to make us happy. So let's call ourselves the "Smith Family Team." How about it if we make a Smith Family Team logo and make up some banners on the computer."

Here are some suggestions for building your team:

- Set up a specific family meeting time each week to discuss family issues.
- Announce that everyone's voice is important in the decision-making process.
- Ask each child for input, and genuinely listen to all suggestions, emphasizing that each person's point of view needs to be respected and considered.
- Acknowledge that you appreciate everyone's help.
- Instead of asking the children questions, talk about your feelings. Say, "I'd like to get your input" instead of "What do you think." Talking this way is important to ensure that the other person doesn't feel pressured or blamed. Questions can put people on the defensive; it's best to find another way to express what you want to say.
- Reinforce each child's contribution and thank him or her for trying and cooperating. ("I appreciate the job you did"; "I'm glad you are trying.")
- Be flexible. The best outcomes will emerge over time, through trial and error.

Everyone's point of view is important and family members need to respect one another to make a successful team.

28. Have Regular Family Meetings

One of the best ways to build a collaborative decision-making process at home is to have regular family meetings. Family meetings can be a valuable time during which everyone can share thoughts and feelings with each other and collaborate on decisions. Having a specified family meeting time will help everyone think of the family as a team.

It takes time and patience to work a family meeting time into everyone's routines. Start working on it as soon as you can when the children are younger. That way, it will be accepted as a regular part of family life. As your children grow, you can increase the length of the meeting and take on more sophisticated subjects for discussion, but the basic principles remain the same.

Below are some suggestions for instituting family meetings:

- Work out a time that's convenient for everyone, deciding on the length of the meeting and where it will be held.

- Develop rules for the family meeting, such as attendance requirements, how younger children will be accommodated, etc.

- Create an agenda by posting a piece of paper on the refrigerator and encouraging everyone to suggest a topic for discussion.

- At the family meeting, each member selects a discussion topic, and each week a new member goes first. Any topics not discussed get put on the next week's agenda.

- Explain that each person needs to open with a positive statement ("I had a good week"; "I got a good grade"; "I liked the way Johnny cleaned his room"; etc.).

- It's important that only one person talk at a time. If others interrupt to talk, it gets out of hand and the person talking will feel frustrated.

- Agree that criticism is not allowed. Model for everyone how acknowledging feelings can replace criticism. (Instead of saying, "You don't listen to me when I tell you to leave my room," say "I feel bad that you won't leave my room when I want privacy.")

- Designate a specific person to listen and ackowledge the feelings of the person speaking. This helps the speaker clarify her feelings better and feel understood.

- The person who speaks next has to summarize what the previous person said before stating what he or she has to say.

- All decisions should be made by consensus. Parents make final decisions by taking into account group consensus (if there is one).

- Once a decision is made, it's written down and everyone gets a copy, or it's posted in a common area.

- Decisions can't be changed until it is discussed at the next family meeting. (There is an exception: if a decision isn't working at all, dad or mom can change it, but this change has to be discussed at the next meeting.)

Family meetings can be used to solve disputes and create better ways of coping. They can also be used to further the idea of teamwork by devoting time during each meeting to coming up with new and creative ways to work as a team.

Once you establish the habit of holding family meetings, you'll be teaching your children the value of collaborative decision making, helping everyone feel as if his or her needs are being attended to and respected, and making your family run more smoothly.

29. Be Realistic about Household Chores

Is there a household in which parents and children don't struggle over household chores? As single parents, you may be especially vulnerable to feeling hurt when your children are uncooperative. After all, you work so hard that your children's refusal to help feels like a terrible betrayal. It's best to consider the whole topic from a fresh perspective.

First, it's important to be realistic. Everyone in your family is busy with important activities. Then it's best to start a household routine when your children are young and cooperative. Remember, though, to prevent your expectations from getting too high. Young children may be eager to help, but are slow and not terribly efficient or thorough. If you meet their efforts with patience and appreciation, they will want to persevere. Always praise your children for their effort. If you become critical and disparage the work your children do, they will stop cooperating.

Phil believed that his children should do chores to teach them responsibility. When they neglected their chores or didn't do them in a timely manner, he grew upset, concerned, and even offended, because it felt as if the children had violated their agreement with him. He tried forcing the children to do their chores, and when they resisted, he became very critical of them. The situation went from bad to worse. In the end, Phil sought professional counseling.

In the safety of the therapist's office, his children explained that they were hurt because they felt as if Phil didn't take their schedule of activities into account and that his expectations of their performance were unrealistic given their other commitments. They said that they felt terrible about always disappointing him and that his constant criticism made them insecure and afraid.

Phil was flabbergasted to learn that his children wanted to please him. He felt guilty over how he had berated them. At the same time, he spoke about how much he wanted his children to grow up to be responsible—and was surprised to hear that his children shared this desire.

Together they were able to create realistic expectations. They also worked out a set of mutually agreed-upon chores and a system of rewards and consequences. They knew that this did not guarantee that the chores would always be completed, so they held regular family meetings with a structure that would keep the meetings constructive. After just a few weeks, even Phil was surprised to see how much more smoothly his household was running.

To tackle chores constructively, remember that:

- It's a team effort.
- Everyone has to participate in drawing up a list of chores and dividing them up.
- Expectations must be realistic and age appropriate.
- Performance improves from trial-and-error learning.
- Positive reinforcement is always more effective than punishment or criticism, which not only undermines the outcome but also the person who is being criticized.
- It's best to ask your child why they're resisting doing a chore. It may be because of something simple like a timing problem. (That is, you may ask her to set the table right in the middle of her favorite TV show.)
- A system that includes rewards and consequences is a good incentive to get children to do chores.
- Use family meetings to work out any kinks that arise.

As team leader of your family, you have the power to make the handling of household chores a constructive and mutually satisfying part of family life.

30. Manage Schoolwork and Homework

From your children's first day of kindergarten until the day they graduate, school shapes their development, learning, identity, and socialization. It's where children become a part of, and participants in, a larger society. In school, your children go a long way towards forging their sense of self, learn how to get along with others, develop their interests, learn how to meet the expectation of others, develop independence, develop and improve their knowledge and skills, form significant relationships outside the family, learn how to follow rules, and take responsibility for themselves. When you consider schoolwork and homework, try to keep the larger picture, and not simply school performance, in mind.

To put your children in the best position to do well in school, it's important to:

- Become a partner in their learning experience. Make sure you attend school meetings, meet-the-teacher night, class performances, and the occasional art show. Volunteer to spend time in the classroom whenever you can. Keep in touch with your child's progress on a daily basis. Express your interest in every facet of your child's life at school, not just in his report card. Children relish the sense that you are overseeing them and that you and their teacher are working together on their behalf.

- Create a bridge between school and home by fashioning a home environment that is conducive to learning. Model intellectual curiosity by reading, subscribing to magazines, frequenting bookstores and local libraries, and talking about your own interests with your kids. Create a special reading area, and later, a special place in which children can do their homework. Find the learning environment that is best for them: some children need a quiet alcove in their own room; others learn best at the dining room table, where they feel close to everyone.

- Work with your children in planning schedules and setting goals. Decide with them how much time will be devoted to schoolwork each night—and then be consistent (always allowing time for breaks). When children are in elementary school, review their assignments with them and help them organize their time. For long-term assignments, help them develop a timeline. Make sure that you are available during homework time to offer help when they ask for it. With this scaffolding, children will eventually assume more of the responsibility for their homework on their own. By the time they reach middle school and high school they will have learned more about how to do it alone.

- Be on the lookout for special problems. If your children seem unusually lazy or resistant to doing their work, they may be experiencing visual, emotional, or learning difficulties that undermine their confidence or make homework difficult for them. Schedule an appointment with the pediatrician to determine if this is the case.

When Cynthia noticed that her daughter Melissa didn't seem interested in school, she spoke to her pediatrician. He suggested that she request a school psychoeducational evaluation to assess Melissa's learning and socialization development. The results indicated that she had great potential but that her immaturity interfered with her grasp of the material and her relationship with the other children. When the school recommended a resource room program in which Melissa could get individual help to improve her skills and confidence, Cynthia requested to volunteer in the class. This way, she could see how the teachers were helping Melissa and how she could use their methods to help Melissa at home. And at home, she did her paperwork as Melissa did her homework.

Find ways to become a vital presence in your children's school lives. They'll not only notice your efforts, they will appreciate them tremendously. In fact, behind just about every active parent you'll find a happy child.

31. Balance Work and Play

Most of our activities can be characterized as either work or play. But these simple words have complicated meanings. For example, if you enjoy sewing and do it to relax, that's *play*. However, if you contract to sew a dress by a certain date and get paid for it, it's *work*.

If you work all the time, you dread it. If you play all the time, you end up dissatisfied. That's why it's important to balance work and play, whether you're at home with your children or at your job. Both work and play are more rewarding when they are in balance.

Whether you're at work or at play, your goal is to be in *flow*. This is a term psychologists use to describe a state you achieve when you get so involved with something that you lose track of time and nothing else seems to exist. During flow, the "doing" is as important as the "achieving."

To help you achieve flow, rely on those activities you love to see you through the ones you find more tedious. Peter, for instance, loved tinkering around in his home workshop. The hours he spent there creating toys for his children helped him get through his job as an accountant, which he found boring. Melinda, on the other hand, loved her job as a troubleshooter in a software company. The pleasure she derived from her work helped her cope with household chores, which she considered tedious. David enjoyed his three-times-a-week racquetball game. With that to look forward to, he was in a good mood both at home and at work.

Create a menu of play and work opportunities for yourself. What's important isn't the number of hours you spend at any particular activity, but that you have choices. Having something you enjoy to look forward to will keep you energized, motivated, and satisfied.

Keep your naturally fluctuating energy levels in mind. Each of us has a unique biorhythm—that is, our energy waxes and wanes over the course of the day. Once you're aware of your own peaks and valleys, try to schedule your most demanding tasks for those times of day when you're at a high energy level, and reserve play for those times when you have less energy. That way, you will be working with, rather than against, your body.

Try to work at playing, and play when you're working, as David does. During his intense racquetball games, he anticipates the ball, developing a great snap of his wrist and accurate kill shots—though he's more focused on honing his skills than beating his opponent. He feels whole and in touch with himself after playing.

He then applies this feeling to work. Though he enjoys his job, there are aspects of it that are less than satisfying. For these times, he's worked out a strategy that allows him to turn the tedious side of work into a game. For example, he times how long it takes him to complete a data form. Then he sets up an objective to reduce that time by a minute. Second, he sees how many trials it takes to complete the form, then he works on reducing the trials to zero so that the form takes less time to complete. When he reaches a level of performance that satisfies him, he creates a new game. He's surprised at how fast time goes during these boring tasks. By "working" when he's at play, and "playing" while he's at work, David enhances both experiences.

Balancing work and play keeps you productive, involved, and alive. The contrasts in life are what keep us feeling vital and satisfied. And remember, when you successfully balance work and play, you'll be serving as a good role model to your children. They copy what they see us doing more than they listen to what we say.

32. Importance of Play

Play is an intrinsic part of life for all animals—including humans. When we play, we're doing much more than having fun; we're also learning about ourselves and our world.

The essence of play is that it's spontaneous, pleasurable, voluntary, and an end in and of itself. During play, we are engaged in whatever we're doing for its own sake, not for any ulterior motive. Play gets our juices going, encourages creativity, and increases our motivation. It's also a means to intimacy. For when we play, we are free to be ourselves and to express what's inside of us. Playing together is the best way to strengthen relationships and grow closer with one another.

You probably spent hours on the floor with your children as infants and toddlers, jiggling mobiles, rolling balls, stacking towers, and spinning tops. Your relationship with them grew because of your play. As children grow, they don't outgrow their need for play. Our challenge is to recognize the need for play in our children's lives, even older children, and to find ways to incorporate it into family life.

George, for example, a pretty serious guy, never thought much about having fun. He feels most comfortable when he's working toward a goal. He grew concerned that his children, who live with their mother, weren't learning discipline at her house. When they spent time with him, he made sure that they followed the rules. As a result, his children began to feel constrained and reluctant to stay with him, which he sensed. When he spoke with them, they explained that they always felt criticized by him and that it was "no fun" staying with him. George took this comment to heart. He realized that he couldn't remember the last time he had actually played with them. The next time his children visited, he told them that he had no plans for the day—they'd just play whatever the children wanted. The children were delighted and, after a number of visits like this, they began to look forward to visiting their dad because they knew that part of each visit would be playtime. Even George realized how much more fun the weekends had become.

Alice, the custodial parent of two young children, also needed to recognize the true value of play. She devoted plenty of time to "fun" activities, taking her children to museums, historical sites, and cultural and community activities. They were also registered for many sports and lessons. One Saturday a snowstorm cancelled the long list of the day's activities. Alice and her family were housebound, and she wasn't sure how they'd survive the day with nothing to do. But the children went down to the basement and found a cache of games and toys from years ago. They ended up having so much fun that Alice decided to devote a part of every weekend to unstructured and spontaneous play. Her children looked forward to it as much as she did.

Play is an essential part of children's lives. Through play, they:

- improve their physical development and coordination, problem-solving skills, and language and cognitive development;
- try out their interpersonal skills;
- gain knowledge of self and others in a safe environment;
- express their emotions and learn how to manage them better;
- find an outlet for their fantasies and enhance their creativity;
- incorporate social norms, learn social roles, and improve their self-control;
- learn how to follow rules.

Play helps you all relax and be yourselves. When families play together, they enjoy being together and feel closer. Incorporating play into your family's life makes your children and you feel good.

33. Play Together

As parents, you're probably very aware of how you teach, preach, guide, instruct, remind, and cajole your children so that they grow up to be responsible adults. But there's one other aspect of family life that's just as important but may be neglected: playing together.

Developmental psychologists have told us that playful parents raise children who are mature, intelligent, competent, and capable of forming close relationships. Engaging in fantasy games with your children, reading to them, and sharing your own sense of imagination fosters their own creativity and success at school. Physical play, including rough-and-tumble play, contributes to your children's social development by helping them learn to manage their feelings and actions better.

If you're not sure how to begin, just follow your children's lead. Most likely, they are freer in their play than you are, so just go along wherever they take you. Become as spontaneous and imaginative as they are. When they sense that you are on their wavelength, they will feel good, and you will enjoy a whole new level of intimacy. Another benefit of joining your children in the spirit of their play is that you will end up with a greater understanding of their motivations and interests; as a result, you'll be more sensitive to their needs.

Here are some ways that you can enhance the trust and openness between you and your children and strengthen your relationship, all through family play:

- Limit how much television they watch. The best way to do this is to make house rules that cover everyone's television watching. You can work out details at a family meeting.

- Spend time planning and structuring playtimes; this helps insure their success.

- Find an appropriate setting for playtimes, and set clear boundaries as to what type of play is allowed, especially when it comes to the rough-and-tumble play many children love. When the limits are clear, children feel emotionally and physically safe, and will be less at risk of injuring themselves or others.
- Remember to include more sedentary activities, like reading to your children and having them read to you, or playing "Let's pretend" or other imagination games.
- Be flexible when you play board games. Older children tend to love them but may not be ready to accept rules or their consequences. In these cases, it's useful to ask if they want you to play like someone their age or yours. Then play accordingly. The outcome will be much better. You can also agree beforehand that if someone doesn't want to play any more, the game will end.

Devoting even a few minutes each day to playing together can make an enormous difference in your family life. Leo, a recently divorced father of two, prided himself on how efficiently he managed his business and his family life. Yet he couldn't help but notice the unhappy faces on his children when he turned down their requests to play with him after dinner. Finally he talked with them about it, and they explained that taking even a small amount of time to play together would make them feel better. After just a few days, he could see the difference—his children were much happier, and so was he.

Having a playful attitude, being spontaneous, letting your child lead when you can, being imaginative, engaging in physical play, having playful materials available at home, and establishing realistic playtime and household rules go a long way toward a meaningful family life.

34. Take Time for Play

As single parents, you know that there's never enough time to get everything done. As you scramble to meet your obligations at work and at home, you probably often have to sacrifice time for play. Yet play is important for the development of your children's physical, cognitive, creative, expressive, social, and linguistic skills and for the quality of your family life. It can't be overlooked or neglected.

Families are at their best when they're playing together. That's when they are the most relaxed, spontaneous, and adventurous. Playtime can also help everyone relax. After playing together, you often feel good about yourself and each other—and closer emotionally. Playing together can even help your family become more stable and secure.

It's certainly a good idea to schedule playtime as part of your daily and weekly activities. This way, all of you have something to look forward to. Spending playtime together can become a family ritual that your children will remember fondly all of their lives. One of the best times to schedule play is after dinner. Your family is already together and can move naturally into a fun family activity. Playing a word or board game, drawing together, or just throwing a ball around for a half-hour each night keeps you feeling connected. Because these activities are fun, your children will look forward to them. Knowing that they will have this time with you each day will ease them through any separation anxieties they may experience when away from you. Finally, playing together at this particular time helps ease difficulties that sometimes arise as children make the transition to evening activities—doing their homework and preparing for bed.

You may have to work hard to schedule playtime, but it's worth the effort. Beth, for instance, had to make many adjustments in her planning in order to accommodate a play hour. First, she asked her children to limit themselves to one after-school activity a week. Then, though she loved to cook, she planned only dinners that were easy and quick to prepare. This freed up an hour two evenings a week, right before bed, when the family could play a game or read together. Her children agreed that they'd get into their pajamas in advance and that no one would answer the phone during this time. Having these evenings to look forward to made everyone happy. She noticed that there was less conflict in the house and that both she and the children were much more willing to cooperate with each other.

It's also important to be alert to the opportunities for spontaneous play that arise every day. Jill, for example, wanted to schedule a regular playtime but couldn't find a free hour. Instead, she purchased a batch of easy-to-set-up toys and games; she also stocked the playroom with playing cards, paper, drawing materials, and clay. This way, she was prepared whenever her children felt like playing. She also encouraged them to play word, fantasy, and storytelling games with her while doing other activities, like driving to the supermarket or waiting in the doctor's office.

Be realistic about what suits your family's time constraints and temperament—but be creative as well. Setting aside even a short play period each week can make the difference between a quarrelsome family and one that enjoys each other. Play can make all the difference.

35. Create a Special Playtime with Each Child

Children feel special when they are singled out, and these good feelings help foster family harmony. When they have your undivided attention without interruption, your children feel good about themselves and secure in their relationship with you. One way to do that is by creating *special times* for play with each child. They learn to express what's inside, feel more in control, and work out the issues in their relationships with you and others through this special playtime. When your children play with you in this special way, it enhances their closeness with you, and it improves their feelings of security. You, in turn, feel even better and closer to them, understand them better, develop a more trustful relationship with them, and feel better about yourself as a result of these special one-on-one playtimes.

These one-on-one playtimes become very special for you and your child. You both look forward to it and the primary benefit is to enhance the competence of each of your children and your closeness with each other. Though it will take some planning to schedule time each week for family group play and one-on-one play, you will be tremendously rewarded by the quality of life that evolves over time for you and your children.

Here are some important tips about how to schedule and create fun one-on-one playtimes:

- Be sure to include your children in all decisions. Start by asking them whether they want to spend a special playtime with just you. Then, mutually agree on a play area; it should be an area in the house where they feel comfortable letting loose, but also where you won't have to impose too many restrictions in terms of their safety.

- Purchase special toys to use just for these special playtimes. Be sure to have materials on hand that lend themselves to spontaneous play, like crayons and clay.
- Set aside a consistent time each week for the special playtime. Though a half-hour is optimum, your child will appreciate any time that you can spare.
- Make sure that you have as few rules as possible. Keep in mind that the only rules that you need are for safety, comfort, and time.
- When you have to enforce a rule, allow your child a few chances for trial-and-error learning before ending the playtime. If you do have to end the playtime, let them know that you will play again at the same time next week.
- Let your child know at the beginning of your time together how much time you have, and give them regular reminders about how much time is left ("We have one minute left to play").
- Instead of barraging your child with questions, try to follow her lead. This isn't a time to direct or teach her. Instead, let her decide what to do and determine the rules.
- As children get older, you can begin to initiate activities outside of the house, like going to the movies, to a museum, or on a hike.

Lisa decided that she'd spend fifteen minutes a day playing with one or the other of her two children. The kids agreed that they would put their pajamas on, brush teeth, and finish any homework when it was their sibling's playtime. They also agreed to buy special toys that would only be brought out for these special playtimes. They fixed up a corner of the basement where they could have the most room for safe play. Lisa discussed safety rules with them but emphasized that these were the only restrictions. What fun she had! She couldn't believe that a mere fifteen minutes enabled her to feel so much more intimately connected with each child. She also discovered that she became much more acutely sensitive to her children's needs. As for her children, they couldn't wait for "Playtime." Even their relationships with their friends and their performance at school seemed to improve.

After just a couple of weeks, Lisa found herself feeling more playful. You may want to consider your own playfulness quotient. Do you enjoy having a good time? The more you do, the more your children will want to model that. And this, in turn, will have an influence on how they play with their siblings, friends, and classmates.

Working and Playing **85**

36. Celebrate Holidays and Other Occasions

Holidays and other family rituals add meaning and give security and stability to family life. At times of transition, these celebrations help us maintain a sense of connection and continuity when everything seems to be changing. By celebrating religious, national, or personal holidays (like birthdays and anniversaries), we acknowledge and recognize our membership in the various groups from which we derive our identity.

Children in single-parent families often have to share holidays with each parent. Working out the timing and logistical details can prove very complicated. Two factors can help ease what might otherwise be a difficult process: having both parents cooperate with each other by considering what's in the best interest of their child, not themselves; and including children in the decision-making.

To cooperate with your former spouse, keep in mind how special holidays are for children. They look forward to having a break from their regular routine and spending time with those they feel close to. You want them to benefit from the joy, support, and sense of identity that they experience during these times. When both parents work out an agreeable and fair schedule for holiday times, everyone benefits. Try to be creative about coming up with solutions. If your children alternate spending Thanksgiving day with you and your former spouse, you can still celebrate Thanksgiving with them every year by scheduling your festive meal for Friday or Saturday. In ways like this, parents cooperate to create the best holiday experience for their children, and no one feels deprived.

It's also important to include children in the decision-making process. Growing up in a religious family, Linda had a strong belief in God that helped her cope with the adversities that she faced—especially her divorce. When she and the children had to move to a new home, one of her first priorities was to find a church at which they all felt comfortable. Together, Linda and her children visited several churches in the area, attended services, and found out about programs. Then they all discussed their impressions, ultimately agreeing on which church to join. In this way, her children felt very much a part of the process and were eager to attend church. Their enthusiasm and the structure that church provided were a great comfort and help to Linda, especially during religious holidays. Instead of having to create rituals for her family on her own, she drew on the resources of the church and the people she met there. And on those holidays that the children didn't spend with her, Linda celebrated at the church with her new friends.

Sally had a different perspective because she hadn't been brought up in a religious home. However, she recognized the importance of celebration and ritual. She was especially enthusiastic about celebrating family birthdays. After her divorce, she not only maintained this tradition but also expanded it. Each month, she and her children decided on a person or an event to celebrate. These choices had to be important to at least one member of the family. They agreed on a special ritual for each of these and invited friends and family to celebrate with them. They really enjoyed doing this. When Sally and the children couldn't be together for major holidays, they could look forward to these occasions.

Celebrating holidays and other occasions is really important in family life. Try to develop holidays that celebrate your family's togetherness and continuity. It's something that your children will look back on fondly when they are older.

37. Get Ready to Date

If you've recently become a single parent, you probably have discovered that most of your energy and motivation is devoted to your children. It's probably all you can do to make a nice home for them, help them with school and their activities, and earn enough money so that your family is secure. It may seem hard to imagine ever having the time—let alone the energy or desire—to find and sustain another intimate relationship. But in time, most people feel the need for adult companionship.

Keep in mind that while you may feel ready to expand your social life, your children may not feel the same. As you've probably noticed, children tend to feel more dependent and insecure following a break-up or divorce. They may be more needy of your attention and nervous if they're not included in all of your activities. You've probably gone out of your way to give them the extra attention they need. Deciding to see someone else doesn't change any of that. In fact, your children will need you to explain, in ways that they can understand, what you're thinking and feeling. Your kids will feel that you are including them by sharing in this way, and they will probably adjust more easily to the changes you're going through. They will be more accepting of this change in your relationship with them when you are open with them.

Phyllis had a hard time being close to anyone after her bitter divorce. One day at a family get-together, her brother brought a friend who was recently divorced. At first she was angry with her brother for trying to set her up, but soon she found that she and his friend had a lot in common. When he asked her if he could call her, she was surprised to find herself handing over her number. Her children, who had seen her with him at the party, kept asking her about him. She was open with them about her insecurities about this development but emphasized that even though it was important to keep it private, she wanted to keep them informed. They felt better for the moment, but she knew it would come up again.

If you do decide to date, here are some tips:

- Proceed with caution. You may still be too vulnerable to develop a serious relationship.
- Be open and honest with your children. They can easily form fantasies and unrealistic expectations.
- Keep dating relationships separate from your family activities.
- Try to arrange dates during times that your children are busy with their activities.
- If you hire a babysitter to stay with your children while you date, plan for a short date the first time you're out and gradually lengthen the interval you're away. For example, think about having a cup of coffee instead of a dinner date the first time.
- Find ways to give your children a special treat when you're out on a date; for example, you can let them have ice cream for dessert or let them stay up late that night.
- Emphasize how important it is that everybody in the family has at least one activity that doesn't include the others. When your family members respect each others' interests and activities, the quality of your relationship improves.
- If a relationship does get serious, remember to consider your children's feelings along with your own when making any decisions about it.

Dating after a divorce is a big step to take. But remember that your feelings and needs are just as important as your children's. You'll be able to care for your children more freely and with more love when you feel as if you're being attended to as well.

38. Share Your Playtime with Others

We've already explored the benefits of play and the ways it contributes to family cohesiveness. Yet trying to come up with, plan, and carry out family play activities can be exhausting, and the more pressure you experience, the less playful you feel.

That's why it's a good idea to plan playtime with other families, especially those in which there are children who are the same age as yours. This opens up new opportunities and allows you to be more creative and flexible. Pooling resources and making plans with another family also eases the emotional, physical, and financial burden on you. You can also take advantage of resources that may not otherwise be available to you: for example, if you have a ski house and your friend has a beach house, you can enjoy both environments by agreeing to spend vacations together. Perhaps best of all, when you share leisure time with another family, you grow closer, learn to trust each other more, and become more of a support for each other. It's also more fun!

Beth's family had always enjoyed camping out. But after her divorce, she was reluctant to undertake a camping trip by herself with her children, ages six and ten. She'd always relied on her former husband to share the chores with her. The prospect of pitching the tent, making a fire, and cooking dinner by herself didn't appeal to her. Plus, she was concerned that she'd be too tired and unable to really enjoy or supervise her children. In short, it didn't sound like much fun. One day she noticed a sign in the library advertising an outdoors club. She called to discover new opportunities for family fun activities and was surprised and delighted to learn that the group met monthly—children included—to plan summer trips together. As the family participated in this group, Beth's children discovered new friends to play with, and Beth found that several of the group members shared her interest in environmental concerns. Not only did she and her children look forward to the group meetings and activities but genuine friendships took root and blossomed for all of them. Beth felt really good to recognize how much her family had changed and grown by reaching out to other families.

To find opportunities for sharing, you can contact:

- Organizations you already belong to like a church or synagogue group or your child's school;
- Local community organizations like libraries or the Y;
- Single-parent support groups;
- Your local parks or civic associations;
- Clubs and alumni associations.

You can also find new opportunities more informally, by networking with the parents of children your children like to play with. You've probably already met their parents when you've dropped off your kids or picked them up, or at open-school night. Try to cultivate the friendship of those people you feel most comfortable with to see if you have mutual interests. Then you can suggest spending an afternoon together. If that goes well, you can try a day trip and perhaps ultimately a longer vacation. It's best to begin modestly and gradually increase the time you spend together so that conflicts don't erupt and you can make sure you're compatible.

You can also approach people in your family the same way.

Remember, though, that shared playtime needs to be balanced with private playtime. Your family still needs time alone to enjoy each other. Group playtime is an addition to, not a substitute for, playtime at home.

Finding others with whom to share playtime helps you feel less isolated and more involved in the world. Try it!

Part IV

Getting Along

39. Find Common Ground

Openness and trust are essential to getting along. For one thing, it's easier to find common ground when you are open and trusting. You probably enjoy more common ground than you may realize with your children. After all, you are a role model for them, which means that consciously or not, they adopt your values. At the same time, because they love you, they want to please you no matter how obstinate they can be. Keeping this reality in mind can help you through many arguments by making you more patient and allowing you to recognize more quickly that their obstinacy is not really a challenge to you.

It's easier to find common ground with your children when you convey acceptance. Acceptance doesn't mean that you give in, but rather that you *accept* what the other person says and believes. If you convey this acceptance, your children will feel validated and it will be easier to work things out with them.

Martha's son, Jimmy, always got good grades until he entered fifth grade. His concerned teacher informed Martha that he wasn't performing up to his abilities. When Martha asked Jimmy about this, he became upset and defensive. She let him know how concerned she was that he was so upset and that she was confident that they'd find an answer together. When he didn't respond right away, she asked him to think about it and let her know when he was ready. She was surprised an hour later when Jimmy blurted out, "I hate school, Mom, my teacher's mean to me." He told her that he was bored and got into trouble with his teacher for fooling around. She told him how much she appreciated it that he let her know his reasons and that she was open to work together with him to change the situation. Together they went to the teacher, who suggested that Jimmy work on an extra credit project when he felt bored. Martha let Jimmy know how proud of him she was and trusted that he would ask her for help when he needed it. Her acceptance and trust made Jimmy feel better and more confident, enabling them to find common ground.

Here are some specific suggestions to help you reach common ground:

- Be more accepting. Believe that others are entitled to their opinions and feelings even if you vehemently disagree, and practice putting this belief into effect.

- Practice acknowledging the other person's position before you react. If your twelve-year-old daughter wants to stay out past her curfew, you're probably tempted to say, "I'm sorry, but midnight is much too late." However, you will begin to find common ground by acknowledging your daughter's position and saying instead, "You want to stay out later tonight because it's a special party."

- Take "ownership" of what you mean. Talk about what motivates your feelings rather than telling her what to do. Don't say, "Midnight is too late for you to be out." Instead, explain to your daughter, "I'm worried that you won't get enough rest if you stay up that late." Try to emphasize the positive in your relationship by adding, "I do trust you. That's why it's important to talk this out."

- Accept that differences are inevitable no matter how hard you work to get agreement. Even if you can't find common ground, let your child know how important it is to you to continue to work toward achieving it.

By accepting others, being open, taking ownership of your feelings, being respectful of the other person's feelings and beliefs, and recognizing that differences are inevitable, you will begin to establish the trust you need to get along as a family.

40. Learn to Accept Differences

No two children in a family are alike. Each of us is born into a different family than our siblings. We receive different amounts of attention and are shaped by external forces beyond our control. But probably the most important reason that siblings aren't more alike has to do with temperament. Temperament, our way of approaching the world, doesn't tend to change over time. For instance, some of us welcome new situations, some of us shy away from them. Some of us are talkers, some prefer silence. Some are easily distracted, some can focus for hours. These are all temperamental differences that define us as unique. Getting along in a family means that you learn to accept these differences.

This isn't as easy as it sounds. We understand others through our own lens. It's easy to assume that if it makes sense to us, it should make sense to others. It's pretty frustrating when it doesn't work out that way—as Fran found out. She had always tried to handle the differences between her two children, Virginia and John, by valuing "fairness." That is, because Virginia was two years older than her brother, she received certain privileges and responsibilities before he did. It seemed "fair," for instance, that Virginia was allowed to have a later bedtime than her brother. But in reality, Virginia was a morning person and always fell asleep earlier than John, who was a night owl. After weeks of trying to make John go to sleep earlier than his body wanted, Fran gave up. She called a family meeting and said, " If we are going to have rules, they have to make sense. We have to accept that we are each different and then look at what the best strategy is." By realizing that family rules should be determined by temperament rather than an abstract notion of fairness, she improved the emotional atmosphere of the house.

Jackie wanted her children to eat well so that they'd be healthy, and toward this end, she prepared fresh vegetables at every meal. Yet her daughter Kim refused them, eating only peanut butter and jelly sandwiches or hot dogs. Dinnertimes became a terrible struggle. Finally, Jackie realized that she could no longer ignore Kim's vehemence. By reading about children's diets and speaking to nutritionists, she learned that children's taste buds are immature; in other words, some of what tasted good to Jackie simply tasted bad to Kim. Jackie learned to be more accepting of Kim's taste in food. She still presented vegetables at each meal but stayed calm when Kim refused to eat them, allowing Kim to eat what pleased her. Jackie took heart in the knowledge that her daughter's taste in food would continue to evolve.

To become more accepting of your children:

- Suspend judgment;
- Try to see where they are coming from;
- If their level of emotion is very high, then there's a good chance that your child is reacting out a temperamental difference that you shouldn't ignore;
- Remind yourself that children are in a perpetual state of development and will change over time.

You have so much invested in your children that truly accepting each child's own way of coping can be truly difficult. Yet this is one of the most important gifts you can give them, especially if you learn to accept others by first accepting yourself.

41. Be Flexible

There are probably few changes in your life that are as stressful as separation and divorce or the circumstances that have led to your being a single parent. What probably got you through was your ability to roll with the punches, regain your energy, and take care of the business at hand. In other words, your ability to be flexible was and continues to be a vital resource. Being a single parent, you probably can anticipate that change will be a consistent part of your life and that of your family. Your ability to be flexible gives you the confidence to face changes and know that you can find the answers you need to cope with them.

Angie understands this. When she discovered that she was pregnant, she knew that she didn't want to marry her child's father. She had been on her own for some time and had developed a lot of confidence in herself. She had developed a good network of friends and had a supportive family. Yet it was also important to her that her child's father be involved with raising their child. It wasn't easy to work out all the arrangements with him, but she was pleased with how much he was involved during their son's birth and early years.

Now that their son Joe is in first grade, she realizes how many changes had been necessary to get to this point. When Joe first visited with his father, it was torture not to be with him. She could have been rigid and not let Joe see his father. However, she kept herself open and flexible about it because she recognized how important it was for Joe to have a relationship with his father. Angie is proud that she has managed to cope with all the changes she's undergone. She doesn't dwell on the past, nor does she blame others or circumstances for her difficulties. She takes ownership for her decisions, even the ones that didn't turn out the way she wanted them to. This flexibility enables her to consider alternatives when her way seems blocked.

Just like you have to work out to keep your muscles, ligaments, and bones flexible, so do you have to work on your emotional and mental flexibility. (In fact, being physically flexible probably helps you become more mentally and emotionally flexible.)

Practice the following regularly:

- Live in the present; don't dwell on the past.
- Accept that you have made mistakes. Ruminating on your mistakes will only bog you down and make you rigid (the opposite of flexible).
- Focus on your accomplishments. Keeping the positives in mind strengthens your emotional and mental flexibility.
- Take one step at a time.
- Don't let your future goals take precedence over what has to be done now.
- Take ownership of what you can control and let go of what you can't.
- Taking action that might lead you to your objectives improves your emotional and mental flexibility.
- Periodically change routines or the way you do something to keep yourself flexible.
- Make sure to include regular relaxation and stress-management activities.

Flexibility is important in your relationship with your children. Because they grow and change so rapidly, they're probably more flexible than you are. The more flexible you become, just to keep up with them, the less stressful your relationship will be.

42. Negotiate Clear Boundaries

Relationships are better and less stressful when boundaries are clear. Boundaries refer to the imaginary lines we make that define us as separate from one another, whether it's individuals in a family from each other, a family from society, your nuclear family from your family of origin and extended families, and so forth. Boundaries can also refer to hierarchical or generational distinctions, such as the difference between children and parents.

Sometimes it's hard to keep boundaries clear; that's because our need to be close to one another often conflicts with our desire to be independent and feel in control of ourselves. Negotiating boundaries is a process in which we're engaged nearly all the time.

A good example of this is Trudy's experience trying to establish consistent bedtimes with her children, Sandra and Billy. In the early days as a single parent, Trudy wanted to do everything that she could to please her kids. She felt bad to think how unhappy they were as a result of the separation and after the divorce. She also felt overwhelmed having to parent all by herself. As a result, she rarely was consistent about bedtime. Some nights, she wanted her children in bed by eight o'clock. Other nights, she let them watch TV until ten. Before long she felt that bedtimes had gotten out of control, and anything that she did to correct it didn't work.

After attending a parenting workshop about discipline, she realized that she needed to be more consistent. She worked on developing a bedtime routine with her children with good structure and boundaries. She made sure to be realistic and to set bedtimes that fit her children's natural routines. She consulted with them to make sure that the routines would be accepted as household and family rules. To reinforce the boundaries positively, she made sure to spend a little quality time with each of them before "lights out." She was pleased at how much better she felt after negotiating clear boundaries with her children.

When boundaries are clear and respected, we are free to make choices within those boundaries and feel more autonomous. The degree in which we experience autonomy is the degree that we can establish close, intimate, and secure relationships, closeness that's impossible to attain without good boundaries.

Keep the following guidelines in mind when you try to maintain clear boundaries:

- It's important to accept that each of us is entitled to our own thoughts and feelings. When you are receptive to the feelings of others and you take responsibility for and own your feelings, you are keeping the boundaries clear.

- The more explicit our boundaries, and the more clearly they are expressed, the easier relationships become. When two people discuss boundaries and agree on them, they can hold each other to the agreement. When these agreements are not talked about, relationships are often more difficult because you're not sure what's expected of you. This can make you feel vulnerable and easily hurt during conflict. It's harder to feel safe if boundaries are unclear.

It's important to remember that (with apologies to Robert Frost) building a fence can make a better neighbor. Keep this in mind when you negotiate boundaries with others, including your children. The clearer the rules and the more everyone understands them, the stronger the boundaries between you. And this, paradoxically, will bring you even closer, because everyone will know what to expect and end up feeling more trusting, secure, and open.

43. Be Realistic about Rules

Rules are a type of boundary. They are agreements that we make with each other to help us relate to and respect one another's autonomy. But these rules need to be realistic and flexible—especially in single-parent households. If you're separating from the child's other parent, try to maintain the rules that you had before. But if rules have to be changed, make sure to discuss them with your children. Asking for their input makes them feel respected. As a result, they will be much more cooperative than they would have been if rules were simply imposed.

Paul was very aware of the importance of reaching an agreement about household rules with his school-aged children. His own father had been very authoritarian, and Paul always vowed that he would be different. For example, the family rule about dinnertime needed to be changed. On the weekends when he had the kids, eating together at six o'clock was no longer feasible because now Paul was responsible for getting children to their afternoon activities and preparing dinner. At a family meeting, they agreed that after breakfast on Saturday and Sunday they'd review the day's plans and come up with a realistic time for dinner. Establishing this new, more flexible rule made the weekend visits much less tense for everyone.

Here are some tips to keep in mind when establishing rules:

- The fewer rules you have, the better. Six or seven are usually enough to establish a context of mutual respect and address basic issues such as safety and logistics. If you create too many, children become overwhelmed and tune them out. Also, it becomes a burden on you to respond consistently to violations.

- Before making a rule, ask yourself if it is really necessary.

- When you set a rule, remember to:

a. Discuss it with your children first;
b. Make sure it's realistic and fits the way they and the family work;
c. State the rule in behaviorally specific terms so that children are better able to implement it. For example, say, " Toys are to be in the toy box by six o'clock" instead of "Keep the floor of your room clean."

- If a rule persistently doesn't work, reevaluate the goal you had in mind, and restructure the rule. For example, you may decide that your children should go to sleep at eight-thirty, but if they don't get tired before nine o'clock, you're inviting struggles needlessly. Just change the rule by making their bedtime nine o'clock. This will eliminate fights and the need for more rules.

- Allow your children enough time to adjust to a new rule, through trial and error learning, before you talk about the consequences that will ensue if they break a rule. The three types of consequences listed here are in order of effectiveness:
   a. *natural consequences*, which happen by themselves. For example, if your child leaves a toy on the floor and it gets lost or broken, you can explain that this is what happens when we don't put things away.
   b. *logical consequences*, which relate in some way to the rule that was broken. For instance, if your child leaves a toy out, you can explain that it can't be played with for a day.
   c. *unrelated consequences*, which have nothing or little to do with the rule that was broken. You can state, for example, that if toys aren't put away, there will be no TV after dinner.

Most of all, keep in mind that family organization works best when everyone's needs and point of view are respected. We need to agree on the rules according to which we live, or else we live in chaos and insecurity.

44. Use Your Power Constructively

We all have the power to act and to manage our own actions. How much power each of us has over anybody else is questionable. Often, the authority or influence that you have over another person is socially determined; that is, as someone's parent, boss, or president, you can exert power.

But your greatest source of power in relation to others has to do with how important you are to them and they to you. This power depends on the quality of the relationship and the degree of trust that you have developed together. In other words, even when you have authority over someone else, as you do when you're a parent, your true power still derives from the quality of the relationship. To use power constructively means that you act in a manner that maintains or improves the trust and quality of the relationship.

It's easy to abuse power, especially when you're feeling stressed. Phyllis, for instance, noticed that she was becoming terribly impatient with Rachel, her four-year-old daughter. Since the divorce, Rachel simply refused to go to bed at her regular bedtime of eight o'clock. At her wit's end, Phyllis tried to overpower Rachel: she threatened the girl with losing her TV privileges and having to go to bed even earlier. But this hard stand only made the rest of the evening and the next day more difficult for both of them. Even worse, Rachel was becoming withdrawn and insecure.

Slowly, Phyllis realized that she was thinking only of her own need for time to herself and ignoring Rachel, who was also stressed by the divorce. Phyllis decided to talk to Rachel about how she was feeling and what she needed. Together, they came up with a new nighttime routine. Now, after Rachel gets into her pajamas and brushes her teeth, they play together and read stories until half past eight. If Rachel shows signs of resisting going to sleep, Phyllis agrees to stay with her but only for five more minutes—then it's lights out. By using her power constructively, Phyllis has improved the quality of their relationship and helped Rachel be more trusting and secure.

Keep these principles in mind:

- As the parent, you have the power to manage things and keep everyone safe.
- Power is a two-way street. It depends on the degree of respect and trust developed in a relationship.
- You are making the best use of your power when your objective is to create a safe and empowering environment for everyone in the family.
- Use your power sparingly—to keep things on track and safe or to meet your own needs.

You are using your power constructively when you:

- Have confidence in your position or expectation;
- Make sure that your position or expectation is realistic;
- State your position or expectation in clear terms;
- Accept that your children may not like or agree with it;
- Are patient when they object or seem disrespectful in their disagreement;
- Refrain from responding defensively by overpowering them when they object;
- Maintain your position by restating the expectation;
- Are able to let go of the less-important expectations and those that you recognize you can't control;

- Let your children know you're disappointed if they can't meet one of your expectations, but do so in a way that doesn't criticize or overpower them;
- Can change your position or expectation when you recognize it is wrong and admit it openly.

Remember, power is only useful if it exists in a relationship that is respectful.

Getting Along

45. Make Conflict Useful

Whenever people live together, there's bound to be conflict. We all want our needs to be met and to feel satisfied, safe, and secure in our own space. But we all go about accomplishing these in different ways. On top of this, there are many other areas in which our needs and desires don't coincide. When we can't get what we want, we feel blocked and undermined—and ultimately threatened. Emotions begin to boil, and before you know it, a conflict erupts.

The more important the issue in contention is to you, the more persistent you will be, which in turn will cause the conflict to escalate. It's also likely that the more important that person is to you, the more the differences between you will affect you. In fact, conflict is perhaps most uncomfortable and threatening when it occurs with someone you love. But if you stop to think about it, many of these conflicts arise precisely *because* you are so important to each other. Just the fact that you get upset and argue with each other is a way of saying, "I care about you."

Children are good at creating conflict just to know that you care. Jesse's mom becomes very businesslike at home when she has to meet a work deadline; it's her way of trying to get everything done. But Jesse ends up feeling ignored. His solution? He does something to upset his mother. Of course, she gets frustrated and angry with him and may even discipline him. But instead of feeling upset, Jesse feels relieved. By getting his mother's attention in this way—even though it's negative attention—he can reassure himself that she still loves and cares about him. In fact, in many families, it's not the source of the conflict that's the problem, but rather the need for attention and reassurance that one is loved.

No matter how painful conflict may be, the answer isn't to avoid it—however much you may want to. In fact, one of the most dangerous ways for a relationship or family to operate is to pursue "peace at any price," because in fact the price is huge.

Since conflict is inevitable, you have to work very hard to avoid it, which often means avoiding the person who's causing you to feel upset. Once this happens, you begin building walls around yourself, and the potential for closeness disintegrates.

In truth, conflict in a relationship is a healthy sign. It can even be helpful, especially if you work out your differences because of it. Airing your differences is a way of finding out whose needs aren't being met. It's a sign that the family is alive, growing, and developing.

You can make conflict useful by:

- Recognizing that the conflict may arise because the structure (the time or place) is not realistic and that changing the structure will lend to a constructive outcome;
- Talking about the situation together and reestablishing your connection to each other;
- Communicating your acceptance that conflict is inevitable and working out an agreement on how to handle conflict;
- Making sure to consider each other's feelings so everyone can feel included in the resolution;
- Acting respectfully toward each other at all times;
- Working toward a compromise to help elicit a positive agreed-upon outcome, even if you agree to disagree.

Remember that conflict draws your attention to what needs to be changed, so that you can keep your family flexible and close.

46. Getting Along as a Whole Family

What does it mean to "get along" as a family? To most of us, it means that we're not fighting. Yet there are some families who, despite seeming to argue with each other nearly all the time, remain fairly stable and happy. Other families may define getting along in terms of sticking to the rules of the household, yet to an outsider they seem very freewheeling and permissive.

In the end, each family defines "getting along" for itself. It may be helpful to think of how well your family gets along not in terms of how much you fight or stick to the rules, but rather in terms of your overall stability and how satisfied everyone feels over time. In other words, consider the general quality of your interrelationships rather than focusing on any one indicator.

Lorraine, for instance, never thought to describe her family as harmonious. She had four children ranging in age from five to twelve. Someone was always fighting with someone else. Try as she might, she couldn't make everybody happy. Gradually, she realized how she could maintain family harmony in the face of these disagreements. She accepted that they were inevitable and explained this to her children, letting them know that she expected them to work out their differences without resorting to physical violence and name-calling. On the other hand, she also encouraged everyone at the dinner table to say something that he or she liked about a member of the family or the family itself. She would tell her children how important it is to say "I love you" as much as possible. She also made sure that the family played a game together or planned some other fun activity at least once a week. She scheduled private time with each child to make sure that they got her attention. The fights didn't stop, but the quality of family life improved: everyone seemed happier, and she liked the way the family was getting along.

Think about getting along as a family in terms of principles and methods we've discussed so far. Here are some suggestions:

- Be respectful to each other and of each other's property and space.
- Don't criticize or judge.
- Own what you say; talk about what things mean to *you*.
- Emphasize the positives and overlook the negatives whenever possible.
- Keep in mind the underlying positives of your relationships with others, and tell them about your positive feelings as often as you can.
- Try to make rules and expectations *house* rules rather than *your* rules. This fosters cooperation.
- Schedule regular family meetings to air ideas and feelings and to find new solutions.
- Developing rules and agreements together and being consistent about following these rules fosters good feeling.
- Schedule family-fun time regularly.
- Remember that none of us is perfect: forgive others and let go of disappointed feelings.
- When something isn't working, talk to each other with an open mind and be open with your feelings.
- Most of all, *don't give up*. Let everyone know how important getting along is to you and how much you are willing to work for it.

Remember, each family defines getting along for itself, but the way to reach this goal is to agree on what you're working toward and work together on obtaining it.

47. Getting Along with the Other Parent

Often, one of the hardest aspects of being a single parent is learning to get along with your children's other parent. Especially if you had a romantic relationship with this person, it can take a long time to extricate yourself from the many residual feelings you have toward someone who once was so important to you. And because you have children together, it may not be feasible (nor best for your kids) to leave your ex-spouse entirely behind. No matter how hard you work at separating yourself from him or her, you can still feel ambushed by feelings of frustration, anger, and helplessness that arise in the course of having to deal with each other around the welfare of your children. Rather than trying to deny these feelings, which never works, it's best to keep the boundaries in mind that will help you and your children cope best. That means that you think hard about what outcomes you want to achieve and what position to take to achieve those outcomes. Then, make every effort to *stay in that position.*

    Jeff did all he could to get an agreement with his former wife for shared custody of their daughter, Roberta. However, the courts did not rule in his favor, allowing Roberta's mother to move with Roberta to a different state. In many ways, Jeff never recovered from this, but eventually he came to *accept* that Roberta was too important to him to let these feelings fester and undermine his relationship with her. He acknowledged this as his first and most important position. He would keep this value in mind so he wouldn't go off the track by reacting defensively.

    Jeff's second position was that although he lived far away, he still shared legal custody for Roberta and needed to remain a vital part of her life. As a result, he decided to spend more time with her than the court mandated, to remain involved with both her religious and public schools, and to keep a separate bedroom for her in his house, creating a sense for both of them that she had an important place there even when she was away from him. He also recognized that getting along with his former spouse would be in Roberta's best interest. Though he felt frustrated and helpless each time he talked with his ex-wife, he stayed in position and worked out compromises that met his daughter's needs. As he practiced this over time, it became easier to stay in position, and he found that the time he spent with Roberta was becoming increasingly more satisfying.

Here are some principles to keep in mind:

- The other parent remains important to your children.
- Your children love both of you.
- The more you and the other parent can work together, the less the children are caught between you. This frees them to focus on what they need to do to develop and grow.
- Pay attention to what you need to do to optimize family life with your child. Don't get trapped into reflexively reacting to how much the other parent upsets you.
- Recognize that your efforts to compensate for those things that concern you about the other parent will probably backfire.
- Stay in position. Pay attention to what is important for your children's welfare.
- Work on compromise while staying in position. Then you can own the decision you have made and not be defensive.
- Always focus your mind on your efforts to create and maintain a quality relationship with your child.

Stay in position and you will feel gratified by the quality of your relationship with your children and with your actions.

48. Getting Along with Young Children

Every day of their lives, young children try to make sense out of their world. Because of their inexperience, they may have difficulty understanding things and expressing their feelings. They also tend to view things concretely and in terms of absolutes: black or white, good or bad. At their age, they are not that flexible in looking at the world.

At the same time, they absorb everything around them, taking in even things they don't understand. You may find yourselves surprised by the depth of their understanding and the power of their perceptions. That's why the way we talk to and relate with young children is so important.

Your goal, naturally, is for your children to become knowledgeable and to use their abilities to be successful and happy. You want them to feel good about themselves, have confidence, and be responsible human beings. You also want them to get along with others and have good relationships. How you relate to and get along with your children from their earliest years throughout their lives provides the modeling and context that helps them develop these competencies that are so important to you.

As a mother, Aimee wanted to have the best relationship that she could with her young children, ages two, four, and seven. The period before she left their father was very difficult and most of her energies were devoted to just coping. Now that just she and the children were settled in to living together, she wanted to do everything that she could to make a secure and meaningful life with them. She recognized that it would be hard for them to verbalize their feelings easily, yet she didn't appreciate it when they acted out their feelings through disobedient or disrespectful behavior. However, she knew that allowing them to express their feelings would help them cope with all the changes that they had experienced.

Aimee made her mind up to be patient with her kids' immaturity and try not to get too frustrated with them. Instead, she would actively listen to their requests before speaking. This way, she understood their feelings before explaining hers. Aimee also knew how important play is to children's development. Her children would often say, "Come play with me," and she knew this was a great way to build a good relationship with them. She made it her policy to put aside whatever she was doing when they asked her to play. Even when time or responsibility pressured her, she would play for a short time, letting her children know in advance how much time she had. Not only did her family seem happier, but she also noticed that her children tended to cooperate willingly.

There are some things to keep in mind about getting along with young children:

- Be respectful of their need for independence.

- Be sensitive to their feelings. Understand what's motivating them before you decide what to do.

- Be realistic about your expectations. Remember that your children are immature and often don't achieve mastery unless they have plenty of time consuming trial-and-error learning.

- Develop a family structure that meets their developmental needs and make sure that the family routines are consistent.

- It isn't always necessary to be sure that they understand the reasons for a limit or rule. It may be easier for them to cope with it if you say sometimes, "Because it's important to me."

Remember to play with them as much as possible; it's the best way to get along.

49. Getting Along with Adolescents

To get along with teenagers means taking into account their developmental needs and changes. One of the most difficult aspects is adjusting to how independent and capable they're becoming. Typically, teenagers progress in both these areas more quickly than you may recognize. Still, as a parent, it's your job to oversee them to ensure their safety and to maintain the values important to your family. They may act as if they no longer regard you as important, but in fact what they need is what they've always needed—acceptance, respect, and unconditional positive regard and love. The key to getting along with your adolescent is finding a balance between conveying respect for their feelings and point of view while overseeing that they are safe and secure. Lead them—don't control them.

Child-development experts have come up with a concept of parenting that promotes competence, higher levels of self-esteem, strong moral development, more self-control, and a stronger sense of independence in children. It's called *authoritative parenting*. Authoritative parents:

- Respond to the expectations of their children and expect their children to respond to theirs;
- Have clear expectations for age-appropriate behavior;
- Encourage give-and-take;
- Enforce rules when necessary;
- Encourage and support their children to express their own opinions and take responsibility for their actions;
- Explain their reasons for their point of view and expectations;

- Clearly inform their children about the assumptions and rationales for rules and regulations.

Sharon found herself increasingly at odds with her oldest child, Francine, who had just entered middle school. Although she'd been an A student, now her grades were suffering, and Sharon thought it was because her daughter was so preoccupied with her social life. Sharon had always encouraged Francine to be independent: she listened to her daughter's point of view, was clear about what was important to her, and asserted her expectations and values. She didn't get offended when Francine acted disrespectfully, but rather encouraged give-and-take. She wanted to respect her daughter's point of view. After thinking about Francine's situation, she decided to have a talk with her daughter.

During this talk, Sharon voiced her concern about Francine's plummeting grades and the fact that their relationship had changed. Sharon said that she couldn't let things continue without making some changes. Though there was some tension between them, Sharon said that she was optimistic that they could work out a new arrangement that would make life easier for both of them. Although she said that she understood how important Francine's social life was to her, she let Francine know that she wanted to help her balance her social life with her responsibilities at home and at school. Eventually, they worked out a timetable according to which Francine first completed her household chores and homework, and then had time to talk on the phone. They also agreed that Sharon would check to see that Francine completed her homework and chores by the designated time. Francine would earn extra social time with her friends each weekend for completing her responsibilities. They both felt good about what they worked out.

Being an authoritative parent isn't easy, but if you keep working at it, you'll be pleased with the outcome.

50. Getting Along with Your Extended Family

When you first became a single parent, it's likely that you looked to your parents, siblings, and extended family for support and help during that difficult transition time. Asking for help isn't easy when you pride yourself on your independence and self-sufficiency. However, it probably was wise for you to consider doing that—and you may not have had much choice. Psychologically and interpersonally, becoming dependent on family puts you in the position where at times you may be treated like a child rather than the responsible parent that you are. This creates a subtle tension in your relationships with your extended family. You're glad for their help, but want to retain your independence and control. Your extended family, out of their love and concern for you and your children, want to take care of you and may be offended sometimes when you resist their efforts. It takes some time and patience to work this out.

    Sally's experience exemplifies all the feelings and stress that this causes. When she separated from her husband, her house had to be sold. As a result, she felt forced to move in with her parents. They were very supportive and pleased to have more time with their grandchildren. Since they were both retired, they could help with childcare, given that Sally would have to find a job. This help was a relief for her, and at first all went well. But as time went on, the arrangement became less than satisfactory. Specifically, her mother became very critical of her parenting methods and thought nothing of speaking her mind in front of Sally and the children, which Sally found very undermining. At the same time, her mother was not consistent in her own methods, which bothered Sally terribly. Yet she found it hard to speak up, feeling that she was simply another child in the household.

    Finally, Sally asked her mother and her father to sit down and talk. It was a difficult conversation. Her mother was hurt when Sally expressed her concerns. Sally let her mother know that she felt bad that her mother was hurt and how much she appreciated the love and concern of both her parents. However, she asserted that she needed their support for her authority with her children, even if at times her parents were uncomfortable with what she chose to do. She stressed that without this support, it would be hard for her to continue to live with them. It was tense for a while after that, but slowly Sally saw that her parents were trying to accommodate her requests. She felt good that her authority was being supported. When she finally moved into her own home, she was pleased that she could leave her parents' house filled with good memories and grateful feelings rather than resentment.

Sally's story exemplifies the importance of maintaining clear boundaries when you are dependent on the support of your extended family. Remember also that your parents aren't your only resource. Your siblings, close uncles, aunts, and cousins can be helpful too. Find ways to make it clear to these family members that while you want their support, you also need their respect for your authority. Once that is clear, you and your children will benefit from the security and warmth that you get from people who love and care for you.

Conclusion

Now that you have finished this book, I hope you've gained some valuable insights and practical information. Throughout the book, I have tried to stay consistent with certain values that I believe are important. These values, which are essential to any relationship, state that we should:

- Respect one another as human beings;
- Be considerate of others, particularly of their feelings;
- Be responsible for our role in any relationship and for ourselves;
- Value the importance of the time spent with others;
- Remember that the quality of our relationships with our children and those close to us is most precious; and
- Recognize that the underlying positives in any relationship are our best resources.

It's also important to accept that you are changing all the time. Everything is in process, which means that nothing stays the same. That's why focusing on the underlying positives in a relationship is so important: it will motivate you to create the satisfaction and good feelings that you want to have.

You also want your children to feel good about themselves, satisfied with their lives, and essentially successful. As a single parent, you are probably often worrying about how you can create the kind of family life you want for them. You may feel as if you're never doing enough. But if you keep in mind how important you are to them and hold onto the values I described earlier, you will be doing plenty. You'll also find yourselves pleased with the quality of your family life and with your children's achievements.

The suggestions and methods described in this book are derived from the values we've been exploring: respecting each other, listening to others' feelings, owning your feelings, etc. To implement these methods, keep the values in mind. It's all too easy to get drawn into negative thinking. But that won't help you achieve what you want to. Think positively, draw upon the methods you've learned here, and remember the values that underlie all important relationships.

This may not come naturally—not at first. You may have to work hard toward the goal. But it will be well worth it in the end.

Barry G. Ginsberg, Ph.D., has been a practicing child and family psychologist for more than thirty years. He is the Executive Director of the Center of Relationship Enhancement and Ginsberg Associates, a child and family psychology practice in Doylestown, Pennsylvania. For the past six years, Ginsberg has hosted a twice-weekly Cable TV program on parenting and contributed to a column on parenting in the local newspaper. He has conducted many parenting seminars for thousands of parents and presented workshops and training programs to professionals on parenting, couple and family relationships. He grew up in a single-parent family.

Ginsberg is a Fellow of the American Psychological Association and Pennsylvania Psychological Association, Diplomate in Family Psychology of the American Board of Professional Psychology, Approved Supervisor of the American Association for Marital and Family Therapy, Diplomate of the American Family Therapy Academy, Registered Play Therapist-Supervisor and a Nationally Certified School Psychologist.

Ginsberg's numerous publications emphasize clinical and preventive interventions with children, couples and families. His previous book is *Relationship Enhancement Family Therapy* (John Wiley & Sons).

Foreword writer **Roberta Israeloff** is the author of four books of personal nonfiction (including *Kindling the Flame: Reflections on Ritual, Faith and Family*, Simon and Schuster), and author and co-author of numerous parenting books. She was a contributing editor to Parents Magazine for six years, and has written dozens of articles on various aspects of parenting and family issues for *The New York Times, Glamour, Good Housekeeping*, and many other national publications including the on-line magazine *Jewish Family and Life*.

Some Other New Harbinger Titles

The Daughter's-In-Law Survival Guide, Item DSG $12.95
Whose Life Is It Anyway?, Item $14.95
It Happened to Me, Item IHPM $17.95
Act it Out, Item AIO $19.95
Parenting Your Older Adopted Child, Item PYAO $16.95
Boy Talk, Item BTLK $14.95
Talking to Alzheimer's, Item TTA $12.95
Helping a Child with Nonverbal Learning Disorder or Asperger's Syndrome, Item HCNL $14.95
The 50 Best Ways to Simplify Your Life, Item FWSL $11.95
When Anger Hurts Your Relationship, Item WARY $13.95
The Couple's Survival Workbook, Item CPSU $18.95
Loving Your Teenage Daughter, Item LYTD $14.95
The Hidden Feeling of Motherhood, Item HFM $14.95
Parenting Well When Your Depressed, Item PWWY $17.95
Thinking Pregnant, Item TKPG $13.95
Pregnancy Stories, Item PS $14.95
The Co-Parenting Survival Guide, Item CPSG $14.95
Family Guide to Emotional Wellness, Item FGEW $24.95
How to Survive and Thrive in an Empty Nest, Item NEST $13.95

Call **toll free, 1-800-748-6273,** or log on to our online bookstore at www.newharbinger.com to order. Have your Visa or Mastercard number ready. Or send a check for the titles you want to New Harbinger Publications, Inc., 5674 Shattuck Ave., Oakland, CA 94609. Include $4.50 for the first book and 75¢ for each additional book, to cover shipping and handling. (California residents please include appropriate sales tax.) Allow two to five weeks for delivery.

Prices subject to change without notice.